----- A Field Guide to -----

FABRIC
DESIGN

Design, ~~...~~ hniques

stashBOOKS®

www.stashbooks.com

Text copyright © 2011 by Kim Kight

Photography and Artwork copyright © 2011
by C&T Publishing, Inc.

PUBLISHER Amy Marson

CREATIVE DIRECTOR
Gailen Runge

ACQUISITIONS EDITOR
Susanne Woods

EDITOR Cynthia Bix

TECHNICAL EDITORS
Sandy Peterson
Kirstie L Pettersen

COVER/BOOK DESIGNER
Kristy Zacharias

PRODUCTION COORDINATOR
Jenny Leicester

PRODUCTION EDITOR
Alice Mace Nakanishi

ILLUSTRATORS
Mary Flynn and
Kirstie L. Pettersen

Photography by
Christina Carty-Francis
and Diane Pedersen of
C&T Publishing, Inc., unless
otherwise noted

Published by Stash Books, an imprint of C&T Publishing, Inc.,
P.O. Box 1456, Lafayette, CA 94549

Library of Congress Cataloging-in-Publication Data

Kight, Kimberly.

 A field guide to fabric design : design, print & sell your own fabric : traditional & digital techniques for quilting, home dec & apparel / Kimberly Kight.

   p. cm.

 Includes bibliographical references.

 ISBN 978-1-60705-355-2 (pbk.)

1. Textile printing--Amateurs' manuals. 2. Textile design--Ama-teurs' manuals. I. Title. II. Title: Traditional & digital techniques for quilting, home dec & apparel.

 TT852.K54 2011

 677'.022--dc22

                        2011010501

Printed in China
10 9 8 7 6 5 4 3 2 1

Dedication

With love to Bryan, Otto, and my mom. And to my dad, who reminded me after a string of screen exposure fail-ures, "If it were easy, everyone would be doing it."

Acknowledgments

Huge thanks to the fabric designers who answered my questions, provided advice, and contributed images: Bari J. Ackerman, Melissa Averinos, Mo Bedell, Michelle Engel Bencsko, Melanie Bowles, Alice Burrows, Amy Butler, Jasonda Desmond, Jan Dicintio, Roisin Fagan, Julie Freimuth, Anna Maria Horner, Heidi Kenney, Bill Kerr, Arounna Khounnoraj, Josephine Kimberling, Jessica Levitt, Jay McCarroll, Erin McMorris, Kathy Miller, Nancy Mims, Heather Moore, Jennifer Moore, Jenean Morrison, Tula Pink, Amy Prior, Weeks Ringle, Denyse Schmidt, Carly Schwerdt, Harmony Susalla, and Jessica Swift.

Thanks to the companies and individuals who donated fab-rics to be featured in the book: Alexander Henry Fabrics, Andreas Becker of Stoff-Schmie.de, Patricia Bravo and Art Gallery Fabrics, Cynthia Mann of Birch Fabrics and Fabricworm, Sharon Lang and Dharma Trading Company, Rysa Pitner and Fabric on Demand, Liza Prior Lucy of Glorious Color, Paula Smail of Henry Road, Lissa Alexander and Moda Fabrics, P&B Textiles, Robert Kaufman Fabrics, and Leslie Bonnell of the Stitch Lab in Austin, Texas.

Several people provided valuable insights and access into their corners of the fabric industry, for which I am eternally grateful: Lisa Denney at Timeless Treasures Fabrics; Stephen Fraser of Spoonflower; Lisa Knowlton; Heather K. Powers; Kyle Sanchez, Emmie Goldenbaum, and Allie Heath of Robert Kaufman Fabrics; Tricia Schmidt; Mallory Theiss; Rhianna White and Bob Ruggiero of Quilts, Inc.; Jessica Willett; and Kelly Wood.

My undying gratitude to everyone at C&T Publishing for helping this book come to life.

Thanks to Kathy Mack, Susan Beal, and Hillary Lang for the general encouragement!

And extra special thanks to everyone who has read and participated in www.TrueUp.net; to Mary Beth Eastman, Kim Steckler, Alexia Abegg; and to the spon-sors who have enabled me to do what I love for a living.

Cover fabric designs: *Sherbet Pips by Aneela Hoey for Moda Fabrics; Peacock by Trois Miettes; and Arôme by Nadja Petremand*

Contents

Introduction

Just a few years ago, it was a rare and special thrill to find fabric prints that inspired me to sew. I looked in quilt shops for anything bright, fresh, and modern among the sea of English garden themes, Civil War reproductions, and batiks. Apparel fabric prints in the chain stores bore no resemblance to the ones in my ready-to-wear clothes. I had a weekend morning ritual of browsing for new arrivals at the handful of online fabrics shops. When I found something that caught my eye, I wanted to shout it from the rooftops to all my sewing friends. I knew there was a hunger out there for modern fabrics that wasn't being fulfilled. That led me to launch my all-fabric, all-the-time blog, www.trueup.net.

Since then, the fabric design scene has completely changed. The major quilting cotton manufacturers are producing collections for modern design sensibilities and a variety of applications—crafting, accessories, home décor, and apparel. Japanese manufacturers have begun to export their unique, ultracute, and artistic fabrics to retailers worldwide. Digital textile printing, using machines similar to your desktop inkjet printer rather than with traditional volume production machinery, has become affordable and accessible to all to create fabric designs and see them on fabric. Several small, independent fabric producers have sprung up, further diversifying the design voices. And the Internet has allowed everyone to showcase their products to a worldwide audience and has enabled designers to share their inspiration and processes.

The fabric industry has started to open up. I no longer have to browse for hours to find great new fabrics—they're everywhere. Still, there's room for more variety and experimentation. A *lot* more. If you've ever dreamed of seeing your own designs on fabric, this is the time to make that dream happen. This book will show you how.

This book is divided into three main sections: Design and Color, Printing, and The World of Fabric Design. In the Design and Color section, you'll learn about the basics of both color and design and how to create repeating patterns by hand and computer. In the Printing section, you'll learn how to get those designs onto fabric—through block printing, screen printing, digital printing, or licensing. The World of Fabric Design will get you thinking about designing for fun or for profit. Sprinkled throughout are valuable Designer Roundtables, in which experienced textile designers share their views of the industry and their creative processes.

Whether you're starting from scratch or coming from other areas of art and design, and no matter what your professional or creative goal, I hope you'll learn something that will help you carve your own unique niche in the ever-evolving field of fabric design.

In conjunction with this book, I am launching a fabric printing forum on True Up for those of you who wish to ask further questions or share inspiration and resources. Just visit www.trueup.net/forum to join. See you there!

Today's Fabrics

The world of fabric design is especially exciting now because along with all the beautiful classic designs being created is a wonderful variety of modern fabrics—from whimsical to edgy. I'm often asked to define the types of fabric I cover on my blog, True Up. I have a hard time because, in fact, there is plenty of crossover between traditional fabric and what I (and others) call *modern* fabric. Modern fabric isn't so much defined by a rejection of traditional styles and methods as it is by exploring and pushing design boundaries. Embracing new technology is certainly part of it, but it doesn't tell the whole story. To me, modern fabric is one or more of the following:

Graphic

Less is more. Clean lines.

Edgy

Digital textile printing is the latest and newest, and with its quick turnaround and lack of minimum purchases, designers can create trendsetting, ultraniche prints.

Organic

Digital printing reduces waste and pollutants significantly. Some traditional fabric manufacturers, too, are leading the way in reducing the social and environmental impact of the textile industry by using organically grown and processed cotton and by printing with low-impact inks and dyes.

Colorful

If there is a rejection of traditional fabric design anywhere, it is here. Muddy palettes, marbled color, and strict "blue for boy, pink for girl" associations are out the window in favor of the bright, bold, sharp, inventive, and eclectic.

International

Modern Japanese *kawaii* (cute) and vintage kimono silks, Scandinavian folk, African wax prints, Welsh weaving, and Otomi embroidery are just some of the design traditions that have been embraced and interpreted internationally in recent years.

Graphic print: Daisy Chain by Alice Apple, printed digitally onto cotton

Edgy print: Jessie by Wolfie & the Sneak, printed digitally onto silk crepe

Organic print: Sea and Sky from Marine by Dan Stiles for Birch Fabrics

Colorful print: Fans from Parisville by Tula Pink for FreeSpirit Fabrics

International print: From My Folklore by Lecien

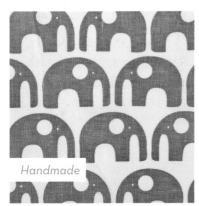

Quirky

I love a print with a little oddness, edginess, and wit—it reminds us not to take ourselves and our creative work so seriously all the time.

Sophisticated

The increased interest in apparel sewing has intensified the need for sophisticated, fashion-forward prints. There will always be Liberty of London (and their emulators), but there is a lot of room for other styles.

Vintage (or timeless)

It's odd to include vintage fabric under the "modern" umbrella, but most people who love modern fabric also love vintage fabrics from the mid-twentieth century. Prints were beautiful, whimsical, functional, and accessible. They're revered today not only out of nostalgia but also because of their diversity and inventiveness in pattern and color. They are also reproduced frequently for today's market.

Handmade

Hands-on printing (and dyeing and painting) techniques are embraced for their beauty, their challenge, and everything that working on a small scale means for the artist and the world.

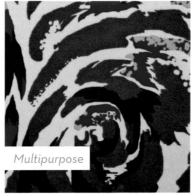

Multipurpose

Base cloths and prints that lend themselves to multiple applications (fashion, quilting, home dec, crafts) not only make good economic sense for the manufacturer but also answer the diversified interests of today's do-it-yourselfer (DIYer).

Beautiful

Above all, it's about knock-your-socks-off beauty—designs that make you see the world in a new way.

- -

Quirky print: Crying Lightning from Totally Severe, printed digitally onto cotton

Handmade print: Elephant by Carly Schwerdt for Umbrella Prints

Sophisticated print: Brooke by Alexander Henry Fabrics

Multipurpose print: Turn of Events velveteen from Innocent Crush by Anna Maria Horner for FreeSpirit Fabrics

Vintage print: Cage Free from Tammis Keefe Tribute collection for Michael Miller Fabrics

Beautiful print: From Hot Blossom collection by Josephine Kimberling for Robert Kaufman fabrics

DESIGN
AND
COLOR

Fabric Design Fundamentals

Fabric design is extraordinary because the artist trusts and encourages others to adapt the two-dimensional work on fabric into a new, three-dimensional form. The imagined end uses for the printed fabric—quilts, clothing, accessories, home décor projects, or anything else that can be made with fabric—can help guide and inspire the designer's work.

Whether you're printing a few yards in your home studio or 10,000 yards in a mill, fabric design involves the seamless repetition of one basic unit over the length of the cloth. In this chapter, you'll get to know the conventions and terminology used by designers in creating patterns for fabric.

To create effective repeating fabric designs, you'll make decisions about the following parameters:

- Directionality and orientation of the design on the fabric

- Motif type (geometric, floral, or novelty)

- Repeat type (square repeat, brick repeat, and others)

- Spacing and scale of motifs

- Color

- Style

This chapter will help you understand these parameters so that you can make the best choices in your own work. Style is the least concrete and definable of all these parameters, but later in the chapter you'll learn specific steps you can take to develop your artistic style. And color is such a complex topic that it gets its own chapter later in this section.

Beyond the Traditional Print: A Note about Pattern

Digital textile printing (see Digital Printing, page 134) is taking fabric design into the territory of fine art. As you read this, fashion and textile design pioneers, newly freed by digital technology from the restrictions imposed by mass production—namely, limitations on the number of colors and the requisite use of pattern—are completely changing the notion of what a fabric print is. Still, digital technology has its own limitations, and the traditional mass production methods will continue to dominate for the foreseeable future. It's unlikely that the use of pattern in textile design will ever disappear, or even decline in the slightest. After all, pattern existed before mass production methods, and it will continue to be beautiful even as digital textile printing makes it unnecessary. Studying pattern design parameters is important because it helps to know the rules in order to break them in an interesting way.

U.K. designers Melanie Bowles and Kathryn Round photographed a vintage dress once owned by a debutante and, using digital textile printing, created an engineered print on silk crepe de chine. The pattern pieces were assembled into a new dress for the exhibition "Trash Fashion: Designing Out Waste" at the Science Museum in London.

Design Parameters

In this section, we'll discuss design parameters—directionality and orientation, motif, repeat type, spacing and scale, and finally, style. If you're not familiar with basic fabric terms, turn to A Look at Fabric Construction (page 99) for a quick overview.

Directionality and Orientation

The *directionality* of a print refers to the number of ways you can rotate the fabric and keep the print looking the same. As you will see, directionality is both an aesthetic and a functional choice.

DIRECTIONAL PRINTS

Most directional prints are oriented *with-the-roll* (with the lengthwise direction of the fabric). If you drew an imaginary line through a motif, such as a tree, from its top to its bottom, that line would be parallel to the selvage. Directional prints can be *one-way* or *two-way*.

One-way prints can only be turned one way; otherwise the print looks upside down or sideways. Even if most motifs are two-way or nondirectional, if just one motif in a design is oriented one way, the entire design is considered one-way. Since this is how most of the real world is oriented, it's the most natural direction in which to lay out prints. However, one-way fabric presents challenges for sewists. This is because cutting layouts for many types of projects are designed so that pieces are oriented lengthwise and crosswise, right side up and wrong side down, to minimize yardage requirements. But with one-way fabrics, all pieces must be oriented the same way, and therefore the project may require more yardage.

Two-way prints look the same whether they're turned right side up or upside down, so they are less limiting in their project layouts than one-way fabrics. One-way (and sometimes two-way) fabrics may require extra attention for patchwork projects. Pieces can all be cut with the lengthwise grain if the project has a definite top and bottom, but quilters may be able to cut out a portion of their pieces the "wrong" way, effectively upgrading the fabric to a two- or four-way print.

NONDIRECTIONAL PRINTS

For apparel manufacturers and home sewists alike, nondirectional prints are favored because sewing pattern pieces may be cut out in any direction, translating to a smaller investment and less waste. Nondirectional prints include two subtypes: tossed and four-way.

Tossed prints can be rotated in any direction, including on the bias, and look the same. Pieces may be cut in any direction, so there is less waste. Visually, they serve as an oasis; the eye can ramble around them in a leisurely way. Spaced, tossed prints often strongly communicate "I'm fun and carefree!" so the designer must decide if that message is consistent with the other aspects of the design.

Four-way prints look the same whether they are oriented at 0°, 90°, 180°, or 270°, and the eye will typically travel along these straight lines. Tartan plaids are one example of this category. Though four-way prints can't be spun any which way like a tossed print, they are functionally nondirectional because most pieces are cut true to the lengthwise or crosswise grain. Bias-cut pieces will look different, but that is usually desirable.

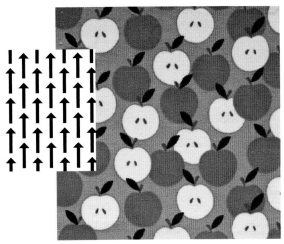

One-way print

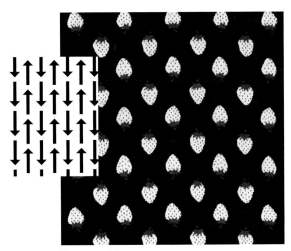

Two-way print

Tossed print

Four-way print

One-way print: Corduroy for Robert Kaufman Fabrics

Tossed print: Falling Leaves from Kanon collection for Daiwabo

Two-way print: Homey Basics collection for Daiwabo

Four-way print: Pears from Metro Market for Robert Kaufman Fabrics

Craft panel

Instructions:

1. Carefully cut along cut lines on both pieces of canvas.
2. Place the two raccoon-shaped pieces with their fancy sides together.
3. Sew 3/8" from cut edge, leaving a 3" opening at the raccoon's feet.
4. Clip where indicated, being careful not to cut into stitching. Also, trim the fabric around points of the ears & tail to about 1/8" from the stitching.

egg press
LET'S STITCH: CLAUSS
www.eggpress.com

designed by egg press
hand-sewn by:

Border print

Cheater print

All-in-one print

Craft panel: Clauss the Raccoon from Let's Stitch kit
for Egg Press

Border print: Grassy Plain from Echiro Fall 2009 collection
by Etsuko Furuya for Kokka

Cheater print: Trefle collection for Kokka

All-in-one print: Petite Ecole for Kokka

OTHER TYPES OF PRINTS

Railroaded prints feature motifs that run parallel to the selvage. This type of print is often found in upholstery fabrics: The fabric can cover the entire back of a sofa, so there is no need for cutting and seaming.

Border prints are railroaded by nature and are designed with specific end uses in mind, such as pillowcases, tablecloths, skirts, totes, and aprons. The decorative border travels along one or both selvages (sometimes the two borders are different), and the remainder is solid or filled with a quieter print.

Designed with even more specific end uses in mind are *craft panels*, *all-in-one prints*, and *cheater prints*.

Craft panels include all the ready-to-sew pieces for a project, such as a stuffed toy, printed directly onto the fabric. Related to these are placement prints, which are not repeating patterns at all (though they might have repeating motifs within them). They might be printed directly onto a finished product, such as a T-shirt or tote bag, or printed along the length of a cloth that is then cut apart and hemmed, as in the case of scarves or tea towels.

Engineered prints are fashion's version of craft panels. Pieces for a garment, such as an apron or dress, are printed directly onto the fabric, with the print already filled in.

All-in-one prints (which are usually railroaded) include a mini–collection of different prints all on one length of fabric. The all-in-one print has come to recent popularity in Japan, and I think it's a great idea for any designer to consider.

A cheater print is mock patchwork, which might be simple squares or complicated traditional quilt patterns like the Double Wedding Ring. The quilter can skip the labor of piecing and go straight to layering and quilting the piece by simply stitching in-the-ditch between print "patches." Cheaters can also be cut apart for scrappy projects. Like all-in-one prints, they are a great way to incorporate several prints into one length of cloth.

Motif Types

The term *motif* refers to any element in a design. It typically applies to a repeated element, but we'll use the term for non-repeated elements as well. It's hard to believe, but textile design involves only three broad categories of motifs: geometric, floral, and novelty. Really, you could narrow it down to two: abstract (geometric) and representational (encompassing both floral and novelty). But floral motifs have been so prevalent throughout eras and cultures that they have been granted a class of their own.

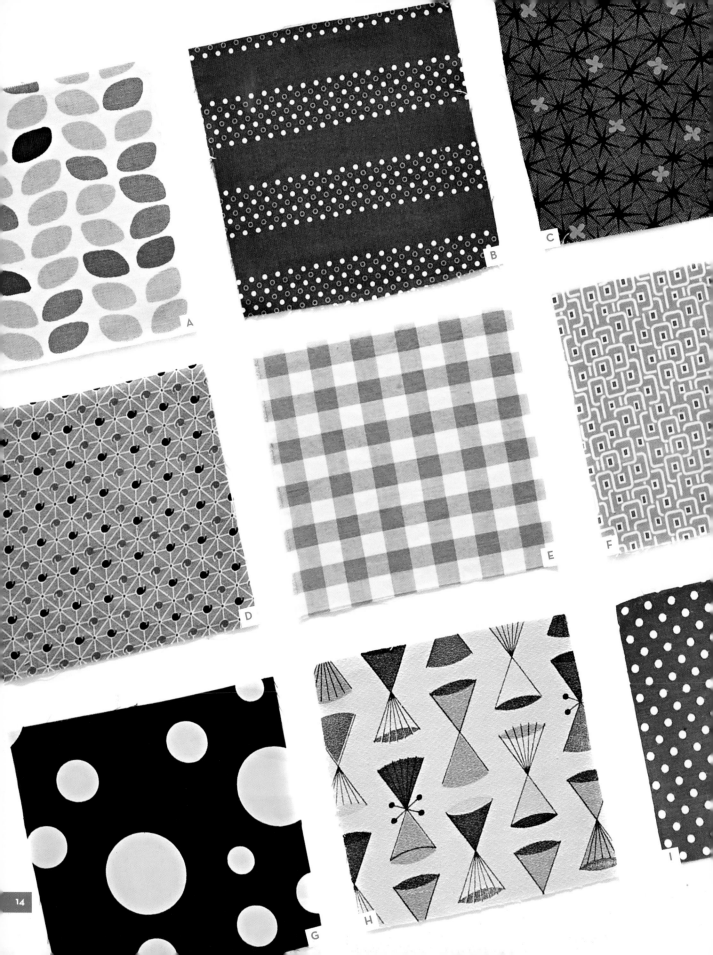

A

B

C

D

E

F

G

H

I

Geometrics. When you think of geometrics, the first things that probably come to mind are the classics—polka dots, stripes, plaids, checks, and diamonds. Geometric patterns can be simple or complex, regimented or random, straight or curvy, or anywhere in between. Some geometric patterns and motifs have real-world associations, but those associations tend to be loose and mutable. For example, tartan plaids originate from and are still strongly associated with Scotland, but they are used so widely that the association is often lost. As such, geometrics are the most versatile and universal of prints.

A. Unknown

B. Unknown

C. Vintage

D. Vintage

E. Gingham by unknown manufacturer

F. Unknown

G. Vintage

H. Vintage barkcloth

I. Vintage

J. Glimmer by Nancy Mims for Mod Green Pod

K. Vintage

L. Vintage

M. Unknown

N. Argyle Plaid from Katie Jump Rope by Denyse Schmidt for FreeSpirit Fabrics

O. Vintage

A

B

C

D

E

F

G

H

I

A FIELD GUIDE TO FABRIC DESIGN

Florals. From cherry blossoms to cabbage roses to ultragraphic blooms, floral prints and patterns are an inextricable part of nearly every design tradition, and just about every fabric collection too. Flowers are feminine, beautiful, and classic; and because of their universal appeal, it's no wonder they get a category all to themselves. And it's a category with more gravitational pull than geometrics—if you toss daisies over a polka dot background, it's considered a floral print, not a geometric.

A. Vintage

B. By Paula Smail for Henry Road

C. Giselle Collection by Jessica Swift for Red Rooster Fabrics

D. Vintage

E. Vintage

F. Vintage barkcloth

G. Lightning Bugs and Other Mysteries by Heather Ross for FreeSpirit Fabrics

H. Old New Spicy Scrap collection for Lecien

I. Vintage

J. Secret Garden for Alexander Henry Fabrics

K. Graphic Roses by Bari J. for Windham Fabrics

L. Unknown Japanese cotton

M. Wild Thyme by Carolyn Gavin for P&B Textiles

N. Medallion Rose from Temple Flowers by Amy Butler for FreeSpirit Fabrics

O. Vintage barkcloth

A

DOG EAT DOG
WINTER DOG
NO BIT
PUPPY LOVE
DOG WOOD
CORN I

B

C

D

E

F

G

racing *down* because this
patterns – you might like t
wkward spaces without w
ransfer *paper*, be careful
ut smaller pieces of trans
rgest motif. Allthe patter
vailable in tubes from all
These dry with a ma
onsistency. Use an old

H

I

Novelty, or "conversational," prints encompass virtually everything else that doesn't fall into the geometric or floral categories. The theme of the motifs (trains, planets, cities) narrows the potential audience for the fabric, but novelties tend to speak more loudly than the other two types, both visually and as an emblem of identity for the wearer or user of the fabric. (And speaking of gravitational pull, the novelty category has the strongest of all. If you throw a duckling in with those daisies and dots, you've got a novelty print.) While several classic themes like old West, kitchen, nautical, zoo, and holiday motifs will always enjoy an audience, the popularity of others can fade in and out with fashion.

- -

A. Lovebirds for Michael Miller Fabrics

B. Hush Puppies from Nicole's Prints for Alexander Henry Fabrics

C. Vintage

D. Unknown Japanese fabric

E. From Vintage Collection for American Folk & Fabric, Inc.

F. From Northern Europe collection for Yuwa Fabrics

G. Peacock by Trois Miettes

H. Unknown Japanese fabric

I. Vintage

J. Belbird by Melissa Bombardiere

K. Corduroy print by unknown

L. Gnomes from Lightning Bugs and Other Mysteries by Heather Ross for FreeSpirit Fabrics

M. Unknown Japanese fabric

N. Hana no Naka by Megumi Sakakibara for Kei Fabrics

O. From Petit Village byTimeless Treasures Fabrics

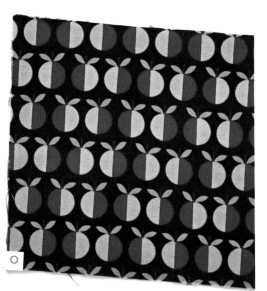

Repeat Types

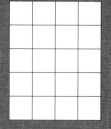

Square repeat print

DESIGNER TIP *A spaced, single-motif square repeat is usually the first type of pattern a beginner makes, but this type is relatively rare in retail fabrics, because these grid-based designs can be visually jarring. These repeats work only with certain styles, motif types, and applications, such as small-scale motifs (in which the "blockiness" decreases) or larger-scale, graphic, clean-lined motifs, like the example below. It's easy to tell when a designer is intentionally harnessing the power of a spaced square repeat rather than just using it for lack of other ideas. Varying the color or some other detail of some of the motifs adds an interesting element of flow.*

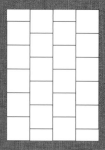

Half-drop repeat print

Snip Snip from Wonderland by MoMo for Moda Fabrics

Brick repeat print

Square repeat print: From Remix by Ann Kelle for Robert Kaufman Fabrics

Half-drop repreat print: From Freebird by MoMo for Moda Fabrics

Brick repeat print: Canyon Flutter from Natura for Alexander Henry Fabrics

Repeat Types

In typical pattern designs, motifs must be arranged into repeating units to be printed continuously and seamlessly on a length of cloth. Here, you'll learn about the types of repeats—square, half-drop, brick, and others. In Step-by-Step Design (page 32), you'll find hands-on instructions on how to create these repeats and ensure that the overall pattern is successful.

Square repeat. This type, also referred to as the block, side, or straight repeat, is the simplest, most basic repeat. The motif or motifs are built within or overlapping a foundational rectangle (or square or parallelogram), and that rectangle is repeated as a simple grid. The grid may be invisible or incorporated overtly as part of the design. All printing methods except digital require that the basic design repeat eventually be built up into a rectangle, so really, all repeating patterns are variations of a square repeat.

Half-drop. Take alternating columns of the square repeat grid and push them down a fraction of the block height—a quarter, a half, three quarters—and you have a drop. Half-drops, where the design is pushed down half of its height, are the most common type of drop and the most common type of repeat overall. Even the simplest of designs draws the eye diagonally in both directions, creating a pleasant flow and balance. It's also easier to camouflage the repeat this way, because it breaks up motifs that, if lined up straight, would cause unintentional striping or *tracking*. (For more on this topic, see Proofing Repeats: Why and How, page 55.) Depending on the motifs, if the repeat unit drops anywhere between a full- and a half-drop, strong one-way diagonals are formed.

Brick repeats involve the same concepts as drops, but the alternating pattern rows, instead of the columns, are staggered.

Random versus Set Layouts

Diamond/lozenge pattern

Ogee pattern

Hexagon pattern

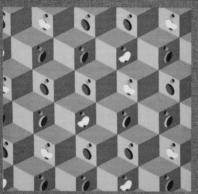

Scales or
clamshell pattern

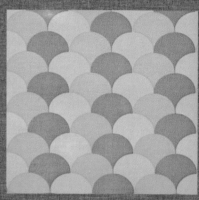

Other tessellation
pattern

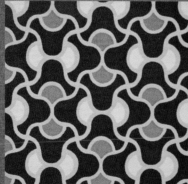

Stripe pattern

Diamond/lozenge pattern: From Pretty Please
by Jennifer Paganelli for FreeSpirit Fabrics

Hexagon pattern: From Nest
by Tula Pink for Moda Fabrics

Other tessellation pattern: From August Fields
by Amy Butler for Rowan Fabrics

Ogee pattern: From Midwest Modern 2
by Amy Butler for Rowan Fabrics

Scales/clamshell pattern: From Charm
by Amy Butler for FreeSpirit Fabrics

Stripe pattern: From Free to Grow
by Nancy Mims for Robert Kaufman Fabrics

Random versus Set Layouts

Motifs can be laid out so that they look randomly scattered over the cloth or so that they appear set in a grid or other arranged pattern. The choice between the two is independent of other design parameters.

In *random* layouts, the most important factor is that the repeat is not supposed to be obvious. The eye should flow over the cloth, and the viewer should have to work a bit to find where the design begins to repeat. The designer achieves this effect by strategically overlapping motifs over the edges of the repeat boundaries, a technique that you'll learn all about in Step-by-Step Design (page 32). Square and drop repeats are most commonly used, though it's possible to use the brick repeat as well.

In contrast, if repetition is flaunted as an important element of the design, the design is said to be in a *set layout*.

Square, drop, and brick repeats can form the underlying grid of a set layout (but see the Designer Tip on page 20 for notes on using the square repeat for set layouts). Other interlocking shapes, sometimes referred to as *tilings* or *tessellations*, are often used as the basis for set layouts as well. For example, take a square grid, turn it 45°, and you have a basic *diamond* pattern. Imagine taking that grid and smushing it from the side or top to make a skinnier or fatter diamond; now you technically have *lozenges*, though most people will still call them diamonds. Smooth the lines of the diamond into curves, and you have *ogees*, which look like onions. *Triangles*, *hexagons*, and *scales* (or *clamshells*) are other classic set layout types. *Stripes* are probably the most familiar set layout type. They are one- or two-way designs composed of long, narrow bands of motifs or solid color. These bands can be straight, wavy, or jagged.

Geometric motifs are the ones most commonly used in set layouts, but motif choice is almost totally independent of repeat and layout choice. As an example, simply imagine a stylized flower repeated in a diamond grid, or a tossed dot print.

Spacing

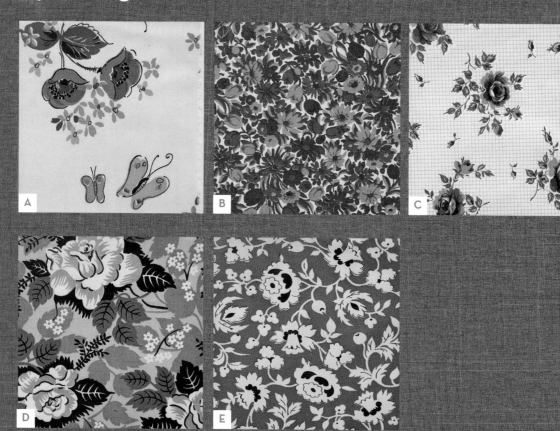

A B C D E

Scale

Small-, medium-, and large-scale patterns

Small-scale print: From Trefle collection for Kokka

Medium-scale print: Matroyska Dolls nd Doilies for Kokka

Large-scale print: From Trefle collection for Kokka

Spacing and Scale

Motifs can be *packed* together, showing little to no background, or *spaced*, showing lots of background. Designs with alternating packed and spaced areas are called *open-and-closed*. They might flow together via *continuous*, connecting elements or appear to float on their own. These are aesthetic choices that don't have strong correlations to a fabric's end uses.

> *Note: Allover print* or *allover pattern* is often used to refer to packed designs. But I've also heard it used to refer to random (as opposed to set) layouts and to distinguish edge-to-edge printed cloth from placement (isolated) or border prints. To avoid confusion, I've chosen to use what I consider the more descriptive terms in each case.

Scale, however, is *very* important in relation to the end uses of a fabric—whether it is used in apparel, home dec, or quilting. Motifs can range from minuscule (pin dots) to the supergraphics popularized by Marimekko in the mid-to-late twentieth century. Though scale is somewhat relative depending on application (e.g., a medium-scale quilting print might be considered a small-scale home dec print), the rough rule of thumb is as follows:

Small-scale motifs = ½″ square and under

Medium-scale motifs = greater than ½″ square to 2″–4″ square

Large-scale motifs = greater than 4″ square

A. The motifs in this vintage print are spaced apart from one another and seem to float against the white background.

B. This vintage floral is more densely packed, though a little bit of background is showing.

C. The simple patterned background of this vintage floral adds subtle interest.

D. The background leaf motifs add flow and dimension to this vintage floral print, as if you're looking down into a flower bed.

E. The flower motifs here are connected with flowing stems and leaves in this vintage fabric.

Developing Your Style

This chapter has covered the more definable parameters of fabric design, but the most important part—style—is impossible to learn from a book. Developing one's artistic voice and style is an individual journey. Like all creative ventures, it's partially about inborn talent. But mostly, it's about hard work, practice, and a desire to explore, learn, and synthesize influences in unique ways.

Following are some concrete things you can do to push yourself forward on that journey.

Cast your net widely. Push beyond the world of fabric itself. Get out of your house, travel (even if only in your own town), learn something new, work in a variety of media—paint, paper, film, music—anything that strikes your fancy. Carry a camera and notebook everywhere. Strive for inspiration from intangibles like ideas, experiences, and feelings.

Set constraints. As you've begun to see, outside factors (end use and printing methods) set some constraints for you in regard to parameters like motif type, scale, and directionality. To avoid "option paralysis"—becoming overwhelmed with choices and therefore paralyzed in decision making—it helps to set constraints. Especially when it comes to the less objective aspects of design (theme, color, and style), imposing constraints on yourself can help you focus and unleash your creativity. Focus on a specific inspiration to guide the way toward a design. Put together an inspiration board. Choose a color palette and challenge yourself to stick with it. On slips of paper, write various parameters (motif type, number of colors, repeat type, media to use). Put them in a jar and draw one at random. They might lead to some genius work, but even if they turn out to be the wrong choices, they often will make the right choices more clear to you.

Join or start a group. Gather like-minded designers and artists for regular, face-to-face gatherings. Discuss goals, share inspiration, constructively critique each others' work, and call each other out on your artistic demons.

DESIGNER ROUNDTABLE:
Obstacles to Creativity

What are your biggest creative obstacles? Option paralysis? Time management? Designer's block? Something else? How do you get over them?

I think every artist runs into one or all of these problems from time to time. Usually for me it's having enough time. But it's important to take a break from what you are doing once in a while to relax and clear your mind. A cup of tea in the garden, a weekend away with friends—having some time for yourself is very important so you don't get burned out and you can continue to enjoy the work that you do. —AMY BUTLER

I think creative blocks are my biggest obstacle, because sometimes I can let fear and doubt take over. My most surefire way to get over it is to just start creating something. Once I'm working, the fear goes away and the creativity comes, but sometimes it's hard to get to the place of just starting even though I don't have any idea of what I'm going to create. —JESSICA SWIFT

When option paralysis hits, I ask myself, Which design idea do I see most clearly? Which can I create by getting the most value for the time I'm spending? Which option is the most commercially viable? and, Which concept fits with the needs I have to fulfill now with deadlines coming up? I usually get over it by answering these questions, creating a plan of action with deadlines, and starting to create! —JOSEPHINE KIMBERLING

The biggest challenge to my creativity is having too many distractions or tasks demanding my attention. I like to be able to really focus when I'm designing, so that I can visualize and be imaginative. In order to keep my ideas organized, I often put together an idea board with images and sketches that relate to the designs and collection I'm working on. Then I will choose a solid block of time—a day or week—when I can focus on designing. —JENNIFER MOORE

For me it's definitely inspiration overload. Everywhere I turn I can come up with a new print idea. The key for me is to make cohesive groups. If I can envision a series of prints revolving around one theme—the seashore, for instance—I will concentrate my focus and begin researching images for that specific idea. This can bring additional overload of concepts, but as I develop prints an overall "look" begins to emerge. There are always many more discarded prints than what will wind up in the final selection; for me, it's nearly four discarded to one kept. —MICHELLE ENGEL BENCSKO

I love planning and research, so the biggest obstacle for me has always been that I think about a project too much before I do it. Sometimes it never gets done because it just never got started! I've learned that sometimes I just have to jump in and figure out things as I go. It may not turn out as well as I would like, but I always feel better once it's done. —JASONDA DESMOND

I never have a shortage of ideas, but sometimes I have too many, and I have trouble deciding which way to go with new collections. If I give myself too much time, I will second-guess myself repeatedly. If I don't have enough time, I feel rushed. I like to complete a collection and then wait a couple of weeks, look at it again, and see how I feel. I need plenty of time both with the collection and away from the collection before I can feel comfortable turning it in. —JENEAN MORRISON

Generally it is inspiration overload—too many wonderful things to work into a repeating pattern and print, and it can be really hard to choose. Sometimes we do a Google search to see if too many other people are using the same motif, but most of the time we just go with our gut feeling and draw what appeals to us. —AROUNNA KHOUNNORAJ AND ROISIN FAGAN

My biggest obstacle is probably negative self-talk, which can be overwhelming if I let it be. I tend to have short bouts of it, but mostly I ignore it. You have to be tenacious to get anywhere in this business, and you can't let a little bit of insecurity get in the way. So much of that negative thinking is brought on by looking to the outside for approval or looking at the work of others and doing that self-destructive, "if only I was like so-and-so" kind of thinking. I have to remind myself to have grace when it comes to how I look at myself, and to only look inside for approval. As I get older, I'm doing a much better job of it. —BARI J. ACKERMAN

Trends: Set, Follow, or Ignore?

It can take a year or more for a traditionally manufactured fabric collection to go from conception to market, and a lot can happen in that time. Of course, nobody can predict the future and know for sure what will be a hit and what will flop. But current trends on the fashion runways, on the streets of major urban centers, and from all kinds of creative industries take some time to trickle down to the public and translate to mass-market production in a predictable way. There is an entire industry devoted to trend analysis and prediction, based not on crystal-ball gazing but on very objective analysis of market dynamics and consumer spending. Of course, the average individual doesn't have access to these services, but you can at least keep up with the cutting edge by following fashion and design media (magazines and blogs). Create inspiration boards or scrapbooks devoted to trends that inspire you. Interpreting trends in your own way is just one way to set creative constraints for yourself, but it's one that can better ensure market success.

What role do current trends and trend prediction play in your work?

Many years ago some very influential trend/color forecasters came by my booth at the International Contemporary Furniture Fair and took pictures for their forecasting publications. I realized that the best thing for me to do was pay attention to what I like and just get it out there. If I start thinking too much about what others think will be fashionable in two years when something I am working on will hit the market (and about what a mass-market audience may like as opposed to a higher-end audience), I just get confused. I'm hired because people like what I do, and I try to toe that line above all else. —DENYSE SCHMIDT

I like to research and stay on top of trends, but I wouldn't say they play a large role in my fabric design. If trends work their way into my fabric designs, it comes more in the form of color than in the form of motifs. I read style blogs and love to look at the latest fashions and home décor magazines, so I am sure some of that works its way into my designs—although it is not something I set out to do. —JENEAN MORRISON

This is a tricky one to answer. It seems like there are so many collections coming out so frequently that there must be something for everyone. On the flip side, there is substantial competition. With my first collection I didn't think too much about trends—it was enough to design a whole collection that I was excited about! Going forward, though, I have put more thought into trends—though to be honest, I am still figuring it out. One nice aspect of the relationship I have with my manufacturer is that they have been doing this a long time and have a more intimate knowledge of the market as a whole and a better idea of trends as they relate specifically to fabric. —MO BEDELL

  None, really. We don't follow any particular consumer trending sites or publications. We want our work to appeal to people and be relevant in the long term, rather than have a short-term, disposable success. —AROUNNA KHOUNNORAJ AND ROISIN FAGAN

 Current trends and trend prediction play strongly in my work. I'm very attracted to trends and forward thinking and am always keeping my eye open for what's coming down the pike. I like using trends as a guide and launching-off point—like a compass—to help direct my work. However, I also don't particularly like to follow a trend exactly, as I enjoy the challenge of finding my own voice among the trends. I also won't bend my style toward a trend if it's not truly me, as I'm all about being artistically true to who I am. —JOSEPHINE KIMBERLING

 It's impossible not to see what's going on around you, so that does play into it. I think the most successful designers are the ones who stay true to themselves and their own personal style. They are the people who set the trends. It's really important to know what's going on, but trend chasing will only leave a designer looking like they don't have their own voice. —TULA PINK

 I don't attempt to forecast or follow trends. As a visual omnivore, I am constantly taking everything in, so I can't help but notice what's out there and be influenced by it in some way. But I indulge in my own color sense and let the designs happen organically, to let them be as authentically "me" as they can be. —MELISSA AVERINOS

 I'd say it's quite relevant. I definitely don't want to offer something passé or so far ahead of the curve—or off the grid entirely—that people will not be interested. If birds are popular and birds are something I'm drawn to, I'll do my best to include them. If the trend was zebras but I didn't really feel an affinity with zebras, I would look elsewhere. Once I spot the trends, I tend to hop off at the first stop and then take my own path the rest of the way home. I think the most successful collections blend trend and individual taste and style: they are those that mesh multiple ideas into one, creating a fresh perspective on what's current. —MICHELLE ENGEL BENCSKO

Copyright Primer

It should go without saying, but I'm surprised at how often it doesn't: *Do your own work.* Copyright law is far too complicated for the scope of this book, but a few myths related to copyright and fabric design come up repeatedly.

Myth #1: *If I change someone else's work by 10 percent, that's enough to make the work my own.*

Reality: There are no mathematical formulas used to determine copyright infringement. If you copy or distribute some or all of a copyrighted work without the permission of its original creator, you may be held liable for copyright infringement.

Myth #2: *I can use clip art in my designs.*

Reality: Not necessarily. Read the terms of use that come with the book, software, or website from which the clip art originated. Sometimes clip art is in the public domain, and sometimes you are not allowed to use it if you are selling whatever product the art is printed on.

Myth #3: *If the source of the work isn't identified, the work is free for me to use.*

Reality: Definitely not true. It seems obvious that you can't use work you find in a book or other publication, but less obvious for things you find on the Internet. The Internet provides easy access to an endless array of amazing, inspiring imagery. The urge to possess these works is normal, and copying is the path of least resistance. But no good comes of copying, and you *will* get caught if you appropriate others' work as your own. It hurts the livelihood of the artist and hinders your own creative growth, so just don't do it. Instead, think about the less tangible aspects that draw you to the work—the lines, the mood, and so forth—and use that as a jumping-off point for your own work. That's the essence of inspiration.

Reproducing Vintage Designs

What if you fall in love with a vintage fabric design and want to create your own version of it? The textile industry is full of vintage reproductions and adaptations, and you might wonder why people are free to copy these designs.

Up until the mid-1900s, fabric designers were usually anonymous, and fabric patterns were typically not copyrighted. Then big-name designers began to emerge, and identifying information and copyright notices started to appear on some fabric selvages. Copyrighting fabric designs wasn't common practice until recent decades.

Today, there are probably millions of yards of fabric circulating that have no identifying information. Some are modern fabrics and their print designs are copyrighted; others are vintage and belong to the public domain if certain conditions are met. Current U.S. copyright law sets the term of copyright to the life of its creator plus 70 years, but works of corporate authorship (a design copyrighted by a company) are protected for 95 years after printing or 120 years after creation. However, depending on the original publication (printing) date and compliance with copyright registration formalities, many works created up to 1989—including fabric prints—are now in the public domain, meaning that you can use them without obtaining permission. See the chart (next page) for details.

The problem with unidentified vintage fabric designs is that there is no way for the average person to reliably identify the date of original "publication" (printing) of a fabric. However, you can make an educated guess based on colors, weave, design styles, and other factors. (For books on dating fabric, see Resources, page 158.) If the work was registered after January 1, 1978,

WHAT'S IN THE PUBLIC DOMAIN?

Date of Publication	Conditions
Before 1923	No restrictions
1923 through 1977	Works published without a copyright notice
1978 through March 1, 1989	Works published without a copyright notice and without subsequent registration within five years
1923 through 1963	Works published with a copyright notice but copyright was not renewed

Adapted from Peter B. Hirtle, © 2004-2011. Last updated January 3, 2011. Use of this chart is governed by the Creative Commons Attribution 3.0 License. For updates: www.copyright.cornell.edu/resources/publicdomain.cfm

copyright information is searchable online through www.copyright.gov/records. For works before 1978, you must perform the search in person at the Library of Congress in Washington, D.C., or pay to have it done for you.

If you want to risk reproducing a vintage textile design, be sure to document your attempts to identify the design's origins and obtain permissions to reproduce it. Should you be accused of copyright infringement, you will at least have evidence that you made a good-faith effort to follow the law. This may help your case, but it may not, as intention is not usually taken into consideration in copyright infringement lawsuits. In short, reproduce vintage designs at your own risk.

And remember that even if you alter the design, you only own the copyright to your changes—not to the original work. If the original work is in the public domain, then anyone is free to reproduce it.

Protecting Your Original Work

According to current U.S. intellectual property law, once you create an original design in a tangible form (not just an idea), the copyright to it belongs to you for the rest of your life plus 70 years. This holds even if you do nothing to notify people of those rights. But it is still prudent, especially if your fabrics will be released to the public, to print the selvage with your name, your company's name, the name of the design, and a copyright symbol with the year of creation. It's even more prudent to register the copyright with the U.S. Copyright Office. At the time of this writing, the cost to register a basic copyright for a single print or a collection of prints online is $35. The primary benefits of registering are twofold: It creates a public record of your copyright that will last in perpetuity, and it gives you the ability to sue infringers. You *must* register the work in order to sue. The damages you can claim depend on the timing of the registration, so don't wait until your rights are violated to file your copyright.

Very few vintage fabrics have identifying or copyright information printed in the selvage, as these do.

A FIELD GUIDE TO FABRIC DESIGN

Step-by-Step Design

When I first became interested in fabric design, I would look at patterns with seemingly random layouts and puzzle over how on earth they were made. The *a-ha!* moment came when I realized that all patterns are built on a foundational rectangle (and remember that squares are types of rectangles). The trick (for random and some kinds of set layouts) is to lay some motifs over the top and one side of the rectangle and then make sure that the parts that fall outside the rectangle enter back into it on the opposite side in perfect alignment.

Repeat boundary

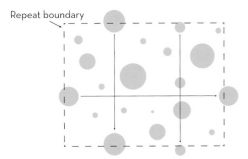

The concept of a basic repeat

This concept is true whether you are designing on paper or on a computer. Though a pattern's internal units might be more complicated, all repeats must eventually be rendered upon a foundational rectangle for printing. The carved blocks and silk screens used for hand printing on fabric are rectangles. Flatbed volume fabric-printing methods also use rectangular screens or plates. Additionally, rotary screenprinting uses plates that are rolled into cylindrical form; the fabric passes under these rolling cylinders and multiple pattern repeats are printed. For more information, see Volume Printing Methods (page 145).

In this chapter, you'll learn how to create square (also called block) repeats and half-drop repeats by hand and on the computer with the image editing program of choice. These are not the only ways, but they do the job well for a variety of pattern types. Creating successful motifs to form the basic unit of repetition is one thing, but configuring the motifs so that they work in repetition—so that the design flows pleasantly when you step back and look at the whole cloth—is an art within itself. After you learn about creating repeats, you'll learn to recognize and repair problems in the overall pattern.

DESIGNING REPEATS BY HAND

In this section, you will learn how to create square repeats and half-drop repeats the simplest way—using paper and pencil.

This time-tested technique for hand drawing repeats involves cutting up and reassembling a drawing in various configurations (it also makes for a cool party trick). Whether you're creating a square or half-drop repeat, the initial steps are the same. *The only difference is the arrangement of the four quadrants in later steps.*

Notes:

- *In the photos for this tutorial, I'm working in pen for clarity, but usually you'd work with pencil while you're working out the design.*

- *Use vellum instead of regular paper; not only does it come in handy for tracing, but it also holds up better against all the taping and untaping you'll be doing. If you are using regular paper, cut apart taped areas with a craft knife rather than risking a rip.*

Square Repeat

1. Cut a rectangle or square of vellum to your desired repeat size. Ensure that the edges are square. Start drawing motifs in the middle, keeping away from all 4 sides of the rectangle for now. Label the 4 quadrants lightly with a pencil.

2. Mark the halfway point on the left and right sides of the vellum. Cut through the center of the square horizontally, starting and ending at the marks you just made (Figure 2). Cut around the interior motifs in spaced designs, or cut right through them, which I did here. (Note that cutting through motifs may involve a little bit of extra work with seam repair; see Repairing Seams in Hand–Rendered, Scanned Artwork, page 47, if digitizing the artwork.)

3. Move the top piece to the bottom, and from the back side, tape the previous bottom and top edges together as they now meet in the center (Figure 3). You now have a new blank middle area to fill in with more design elements.

4. Continue your design into the middle area by drawing over the taped horizontal seam. This time, stay away from the left and right sides (Figure 4).

5. Now, mark the halfway point on the top and the bottom of the vellum. Cut through the design vertically, starting and stopping at these new marks. Move the left-hand section to the right side, and tape the sections back together (Figure 5). Again, fill in the middle, this time over the vertical seam (Figure 6).

6. You may still have a little area along the top and bottom middle edges to fill in. To do this, detach horizontally through the design on the previously cut lines, reassemble and tape the quadrants together (Figure 7), and complete the middle portion of the drawing (Figure 8).

7. Your repeating pattern is now complete, but you may wish to cut all 4 quadrants apart and tape them back in the original 1-2-3-4 configuration, as shown in Figure 9. Either way, the overall pattern remains the same; however, the starting place of the pattern repeat is different. Finished! You can now hand proof the design (see Proofing Repeats, page 55) or scan it for digital manipulation (see page 40).

Square Repeat

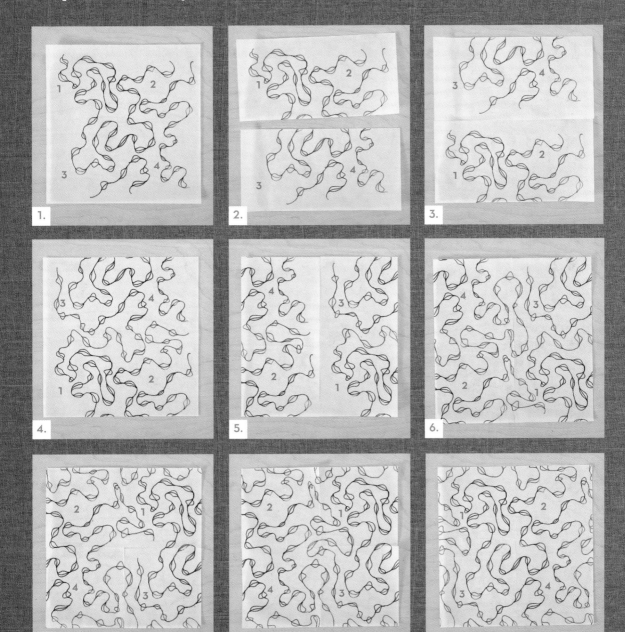

Tutorial: DESIGNING REPEATS BY HAND

Half-Drop Repeat

1. Follow the first 4 steps of the square repeat procedure (Figures 10–13). You will cut the vellum once horizontally and fill in your drawing over the horizontal seam.

2. Mark the center of the top and bottom sides. Cut vertically through the design, starting and ending at the marks you just made, and then detach the sections (Figure 14). If you cut around motifs instead of straight through, it can be a little tricky to start and end your cuts at these center marks. Some funky shapes might result when you tape the sections back together in the next steps—but don't worry, the repeat will still work.

3. *This is the key step in creating a half-drop.* Cut the quadrants apart and reassemble and tape the quadrants together (Figure 15), lining up the square center corners. This configuration makes it so that motifs falling off the top right (side) edge reenter on the *lower* left edge of the repeat, and motifs falling off the bottom right (side) edge reenter on the *upper* left edge.

4. Fill in the middle of the drawing over the center vertical seam (Figure 16).

5. Cut the quadrants apart again and reassemble and retape them together (Figure 17). Fill in the remaining middle space if needed (here, it wasn't).

6. Reassemble and tape the quadrants back into the original 1-2-3-4 configuration (Figure 18). You're finished! You can now hand proof the design (see Proofing Repeats, page 55, or scan for digital manipulation, page 40).

Half-Drop Repeat

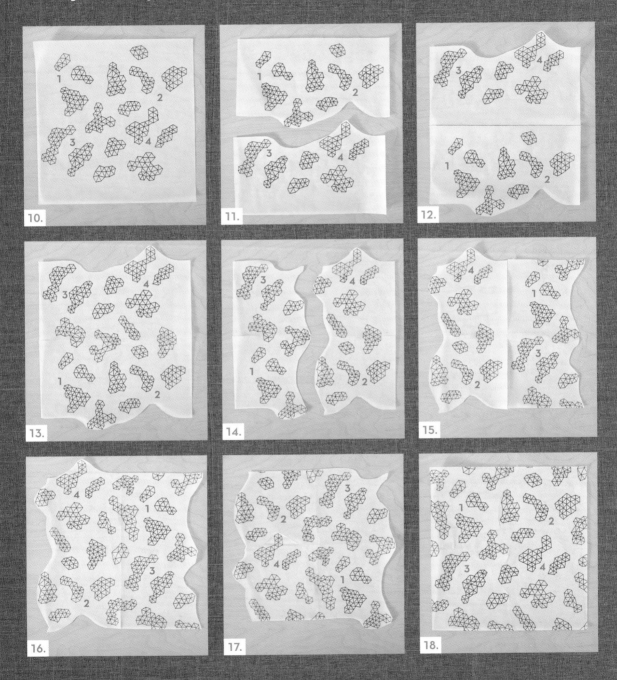

DESIGNING REPEATS BY COMPUTER

In this section, you'll learn how to design repeats using the two most widely used image editing programs: Adobe Photoshop and Adobe Illustrator.

Note: These tutorials assume basic familiarity with Adobe Photoshop and Adobe Illustrator Creative Suite 3 (CS3) or later versions, including basic file management; knowledge of the different selection, drawing and coloring tools; and basic layer manipulation. See Resources (page 158) for suggestions if you are not familiar with these programs. You also may be able to experiment with these software programs at your local copy center.

You may be wondering which program is the best to use for fabric design. In short, both Adobe Photoshop and Adobe Illustrator are powerful tools that can be used for creating repeats and, as you'll see in the next chapter (Know Your Color, page 58), for easily auditioning color for your designs. Each has its own strengths and weaknesses, but either can be used to create a design from scratch or to manipulate and edit scanned artwork. Before delving into the tutorials for creating repeats, here is a primer on the differences between the programs and some special considerations for the fabric design process.

Photoshop is a raster image editing program—it builds images from pixels. It was developed for editing digital photographs, in which areas of color blend together without any sharp delineation between them. A digital photograph might contain thousands or even millions of colors. Though not its primary purpose, Photoshop can be used as a drawing tool (and fabric designing tool) as well. Its biggest disadvantages are that, unless special settings are selected, artwork loses clarity when scaled up and down. However, most people find it easier to maintain the integrity and expression of hand-drawn lines in Photoshop, whether they are working from scratch or manipulating a scan.

Illustrator is a vector image editing program, which means that it creates images from points (vectors) and lines. These images can be scaled up and down infinitely without any loss of quality. Its coloring tools are far more robust compared with Photoshop. Natural-looking lines can be difficult to achieve—unless you are experienced, Illustrator is best suited to very graphic, sharp lines.

What's Your Alias?

By default, raster images—which include drawings made in Photoshop and scanned artwork—are *anti-aliased*, which refers to the blending of color into the background color(s) by use of increasingly transparent colors. Without anti-aliasing, shapes look jagged on the computer screen, as shown in Figures 1 and 2, and in print.

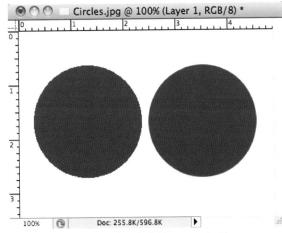

Figure 1: An un-anti-aliased circle (left) compared with an anti-aliased one (right) at 100% resolution.

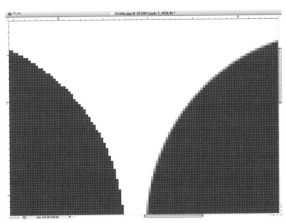

Figure 2: Detail of the circles' edges, seen up close. Note how the pixels of the anti-aliased circle (right) become gradually lighter toward the edge.

The jagged look of shapes is a concern for fabric printing as well. However, the jaggedness becomes less visible at higher resolutions. Fabric is more forgiving in this regard than paper, because it has more texture and absorbs ink more readily. I have printed an un-anti-aliased design at 150 dots per inch (dpi)—the minimum recommended resolution of most digital print bureaus—and the jaggedness is only visible to the trained eye when looking closely. It's unlikely that jaggedness would be a concern at 300 dpi or higher, whether the design is printed digitally onto fabric or as a positive for screen printing.

When designing fabric prints in Photoshop or Illustrator using this chapter's tutorials, you will either work with a scan of a black-and-white line drawing, draw directly in the image file, or both.

If you will be working in Photoshop, decide whether you want to use un-anti-aliased art or anti-aliased art. Either is acceptable for any type of printing process. Un-anti-aliased art is far easier to work with, as unintuitive as it may be for those experienced in print design. However, you may want to use anti-aliased art for several reasons:

- It's the default way of working in Photoshop, with no need to change any settings.
- Some find that it better captures the quality and expressiveness of hand-rendered lines.
- It's far easier to achieve natural-looking areas of blended color, for example, shadows and highlights.
- You want the best guarantee that the edges of your motifs won't look jagged.

Scanning Line Art for Fabric Design

Scanned line art—such as a sketch or ink drawing or a hand-rendered repeat that you created in the tutorials earlier in the chapter—can be used to build a design in Illustrator or Photoshop. These scans might simply be imported into the programs and left in the background to trace over with the program's own drawing tools, and deleted after the process is complete. If this is the case, an anti-aliased scan (scanned in grayscale or color mode) is fine. You can also work directly with the scanned image, arranging, manipulating, and coloring the motifs and putting them into repeat. If this is the case, the best way to scan line art is as a high-resolution, black-and-white, un-anti-aliased bitmap, whether you intend to work in Photoshop or Illustrator.

For Photoshop

1. Scan line art at 600 dpi as a black-and-white image (bitmap). Save the file as a .tif. The resulting file will be un-anti-aliased on a white background (Figure 1). Here, I have scanned the design I created for the hand-drawn half-drop repeat tutorial and zoomed in to show the jagged edges of the un-anti-aliased artwork.

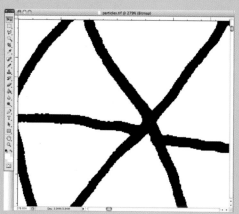

Figure 1

2. Open the file and clean up any stray black pixels with the *Eraser tool*. Convert the file to *Grayscale* (*Image > Mode > Grayscale*); then click *OK* in the dialog box that pops up (you want the default *Size Ratio* of 1). Open the *Layers* panel (*Window > Layers*)—you must double-click on the lock to make the artwork editable. Name the layer as desired.

3. Select the white background with the *Magic Wand* (*Contiguous* option unchecked) and delete it (Figure 2). At this point, you have artwork suitable for manipulation in a variety of ways. Since the file now has a transparent background, you are free to add your own background layer filled with a color or pattern of choice.

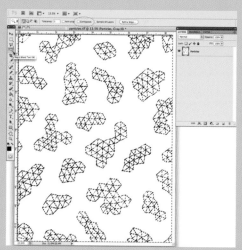

Figure 2

4. *To convert to anti-aliased art, proceed to Step 5.* To continue working with un-anti-aliased art: Go to *Photoshop > Preferences > General* and set the *Image Interpolation* to *Nearest Neighbor* (*Preserve Hard Edges*) (Figure 3). This way, motifs will remain un-anti-aliased after transforming them in any way—rotating, resizing, reflecting, and so forth. Additionally, uncheck the *Anti-Alias* option for each drawing and selection tool (such as the *Paint Bucket* and *Magic Wand*). Proceed to Step 6.

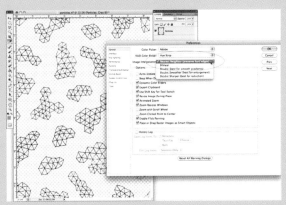

Figure 3: Setting *Image Interpolation* to *Nearest Neighbor*. The artwork is now against a transparent background.

5. To convert to anti-aliased art: Go to *Photoshop > Preferences > General* to ensure the *Image Interpolation* is set to the default (*Bicubic*). Now, reduce the image size to 300 dpi (or any other resolution up to 600)—afterward, the artwork will be anti-aliased (Figure 4).

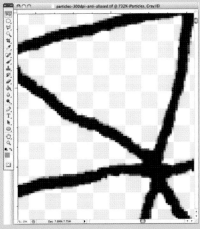

Figure 4

6. Work in the current file if your scanned art was already in repeat. (For hints on repairing seams, see the sidebar on page 47.) If you are creating a repeat anew in Photoshop, you may wish to create a separate 600 dpi, transparent-background file in the dimensions of your desired repeat size and the same resolution as your scan, so that you can copy and paste motifs into this new file, working on the layout as you go.

For Illustrator

Scan line art at 600 dpi as a black-and-white image (bitmap). Save the file as a .tif. The resulting scan will be un-anti-aliased on a white background.

1. Create a new file in Illustrator and place the .tif file (*File > Place*). Deselect the artwork.

2. Open *Live Trace Options* (*Object > Live Trace > Live Trace Options*). Check the *Ignore White* option and then click *Set Default*. Select the artwork. Apply *Live Trace* (*Object > Live Trace > Make and Expand*). If you are unhappy with the line quality, undo and try some of the other presets in *Live Trace Options* or experiment with the settings on your own. The motifs are now ready to arrange, manipulate, color, and put into repeat (Figure 5).

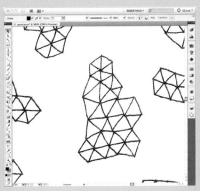

Figure 5: The artwork after *Live Trace* is applied—the art, originally a bitmap scan, is now in vector format.

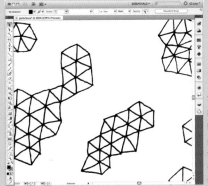

The artwork is deselected here. *Live Trace* preserved the wonky hand-drawn qualities of the motifs well.

Designing Repeats in Photoshop

The technique for creating repeats in Photoshop is very similar to drawing them by hand; the only difference is that the *Offset* filter is used in place of cutting and rearranging quadrants.

SQUARE REPEATS

1. Create a new file the size of the desired repeat. Jot down the size in pixels (*Image > Image Size*). My sample design is 4800 × 4800 pixels. If your design will be printed digitally (see page 134), set up the document to the dpi and color mode specified by the printer. Draw your design in the middle of the box (Figure 1).

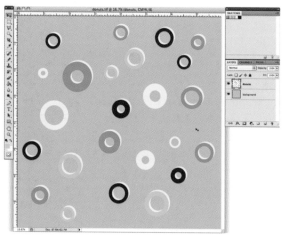
Figure 1

2. From the *Filter* menu, choose *Other > Offset*. Set the *Vertical Offset* to half the image size (here, 2400) and the *Horizontal Offset* to 0 (see Figure 2). Select the *Wrap Around* option if it is not selected already, and then click *OK*. The top and bottom edges from Step 1 now meet in the middle of the workspace. Notice how motifs that were in the middle are now split along the top and bottom edges.

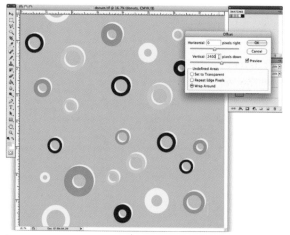
Figure 2

TIPS

*   *You are required to rasterize any vector shapes in the layer (Layer > Rasterize > All Layers) before applying the* Offset *filter.*

*   *The* Offset *filter applies to one layer at a time, so if you have multiple layers, you must either merge them before applying the filter (Layer > Merge Layers) or offset each individually. If the background is a solid color, there is no need to offset it.*

3. Fill in the middle with motifs (by adding new motifs or rearranging existing ones), *staying away from the left and right sides* (Figure 3).

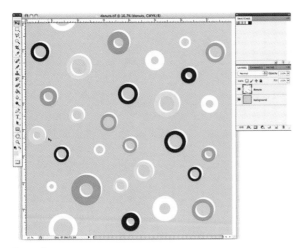

Figure 3

4. Reapply the *Offset* filter (*Filter > Other > Offset*), this time with the *Horizontal Offset* set to half of the image width (here it is 2400) and the *Vertical Offset* set back to 0. Select the *Wrap Around* option if it is not selected already, and then click *OK* (Figure 4). Now, the left and right edges from Step 1 are brought into the center of the workspace.

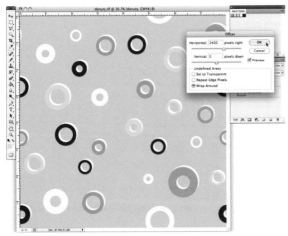

Figure 4

5. Fill in the middle again with motifs, this time staying away from the top and bottom middle edges (Figure 5).

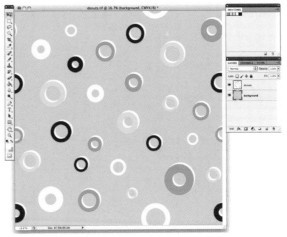

Figure 5

6. At this point, some designs will still have a gap in the area where the 4 outside corners of the repeat from Step 1 meet. Apply the *Offset* filter once more (*Filter > Other > Offset*), this time with the *Vertical Offset* set to half the image height (here it is 2400) and the *Horizontal Offset* set to 0 (Figure 6). This brings those 4 corners together into the center of the workspace.

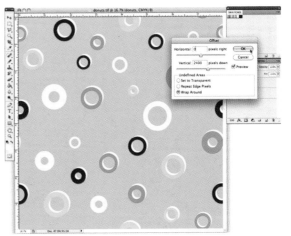

Figure 6

7. If needed, fill in the last bit of the design. When you're finished, set the *Horizontal Offset* and *Vertical Offset* filters back to 0 if desired, but the design will now repeat seamlessly no matter if it's offset from its original position or not. If you end up being happy with the design in repeat, this is the completed file you would send to a digital print bureau, fabric manufacturer, and so on.

8. Now, you will "proof" the pattern, checking that the pattern swatch you just created tiles seamlessly and that the repeat flows well. From the *Edit* menu, choose *Define Pattern*, and name the pattern. Create a new file with a canvas size at least 300% of the original repeat size. Choose *Edit > Fill*. From the popup menu under *Use*, choose *Pattern,* and locate the pattern you just saved. Click on it to fill your workspace (Figure 7). If you like what you see, you are finished! (See page 47 for more on proofing and repairing patterns so that you know what to look for and how to repair the pattern if you *don't* like what you see.)

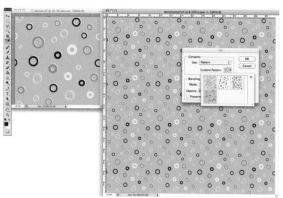

Figure 7: The final design after some further edits (left) and its proof (right)

HALF-DROP REPEATS

1. Complete Steps 1 and 2 of the Photoshop Square Repeats (page 42). Your design is now in repeat along the top and bottom edges, but not yet on the sides.

2. Convert the layer(s) containing your motifs to a *Smart Object (Layer > Smart Object > Convert to Smart Object)*. This will allow the copies you are about to make to snap into perfect alignment. Also, pull a horizontal guide down and place it exactly in the middle of the design (*View > Rulers*; then click and drag from the ruler area).

3. As shown in Figure 8, increase the *Canvas Size (Image > Canvas Size)* 200% in both width and height. In the *Canvas Size* options, *Anchor* the canvas center left and center.

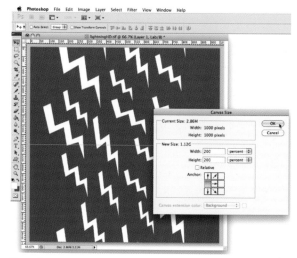

Figure 8

4. Create 2 duplicate layers of your design (*Layer > Duplicate Layer*) and move them above and below the original design, as shown in Figure 9, ensuring that they are in perfect alignment with no overlap or gaps. They will snap into place because the original layer is a *Smart Object*. Half of each new layer will fall outside the canvas boundaries. Add a vertical guide at the right-hand edge of the pattern (here, it is at 1000 pixels on the ruler).

44

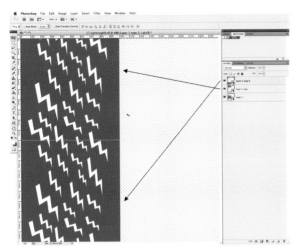

Figure 9

5. Make 2 more copies of the original layer, this time dragging the new layers to the top and bottom right, as shown. One new layer is placed above the original center horizontal guide and one is placed below. Now, place 2 more guides horizontally, which bisect the new layers on the right (Figure 10).

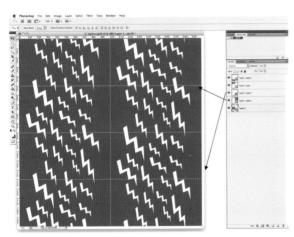

Figure 10

6. Fill the middle area with motifs between the top and bottom horizontal guides, leaving some space near the guides themselves. Then, crop the middle so that it contains exactly the original layer on the left, the bottom half of the top-right layer, and the top half of the bottom-right

layer (Figure 11). (Using the *Crop* tool, click in the upper left corner near the arrowhead and drag to the lower right corner. The shaded areas on the screenshot will be cropped out.)

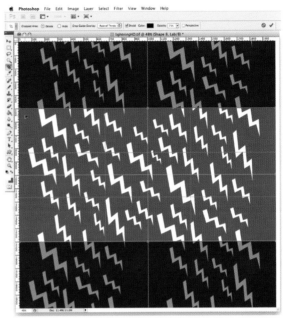

Figure 11

7. Select all layers and merge them into one layer (*Layer > Merge Layers*). Apply the *Offset* filter (*Filter > Other > Offset*), setting the *Vertical Offset* to half the original size (here it is 500 pixels) and the *Horizontal Offset* to 0 (Figure 12). Be sure the *Wrap Around* option is selected.

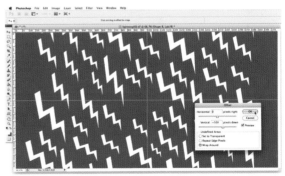

Figure 12

8. Fill in the last remaining empty area, which is now positioned in the middle of the window (Figure 13), with more motifs. Some designs will not require this step.

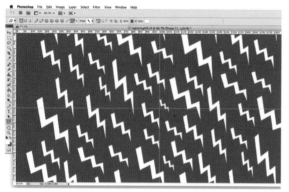

Figure 13

9. Choose the *Rectangular Marquee* tool and set its style to *Fixed Size,* and set the size the same as the original repeat size (here it is 1000 × 1000 pixels). Click in the workspace window and position the marquee in the exact center vertically (Figure 14). Horizontal positioning is not crucial at this point, as long as the marquee falls roughly in the middle of your design.

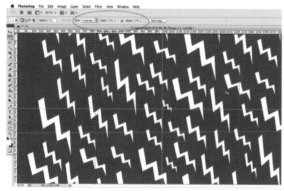

Figure 14

10. From the *Image* menu, choose *Crop,* then *Select > Deselect.* The basic repeat is finished (Figure 15). If you wish to use Photoshop's *Define Pattern* function to proof the pattern, however, you must build it up into a square repeat. Simply rebuild the configuration of duplicate layers you made in Steps 1–3, only using the completed repeat. Then, follow Step 8 in the Square Repeats tutorial to define and proof the pattern. Figure 16 shows the proofed design.

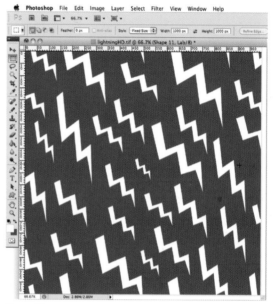

Figure 15

Figure 16

Tutorial: DESIGNING REPEATS BY COMPUTER

Repairing Seams in Hand-Rendered, Scanned Artwork

You may wish to scan the hand-rendered repeats for digital manipulation or printing. If you cut through motifs (as I did in the Square Repeats tutorial, page 34), you will need to repair the seams (most easily achieved in Photoshop) before proceeding with editing or coloring. Place the document as squarely as possible on the scanner—any skew will make seam repair more difficult. Scan according to your preferred specifications (discussed on page 40). Open the document in Photoshop, and pull down horizontal guides to help you see if your design is square. Rotate and crop if necessary to make the design as straight as possible.

Note the image size in pixels. From the *Filter* menu, choose *Other > Offset*. Set the *Vertical Offset* to half the image size and keep the *Horizontal Offset* at 0. This will bring the top and bottom seams together in the middle of the canvas. Use Photoshop's drawing and retouching tools (such as the *Eraser* and *Rubber Stamp*) to eliminate any seamlines in the background and to bring misaligned motifs back together. When finished, repeat the application of the *Offset* filter, this time setting the *Horizontal Offset* to half the image size and the *Vertical Offset* to 0. Repair the side seams, which will now be brought together in the center of the canvas.

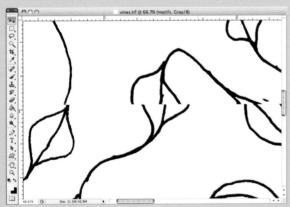

After applying the *Offset* filter, poor alignment along the seams is evident.

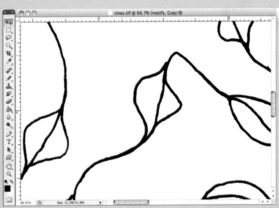

The same portion of the design after repairing. Because the art is un-anti-aliased, I was able simply to redraw the lines with the *Pencil* tool and erase the old lines with the *Eraser* tool.

Designing Repeats in Illustrator

Adobe Illustrator doesn't have the exact equivalent to Photoshop's *Offset* filter, but it does have powerful alignment tools that allow you to position copies of motifs precisely upon the repeat boundaries. When creating a square repeat, for every motif that leaves the repeat boundaries, you will create a copy and align it with the original on the opposite side of a bounding box. The tiling steps you need to build a half-drop repeat are basically the same as they are in Photoshop.

> *Note: Here, I am creating a set layout of ogees, but the same principles apply to random layouts.*

SQUARE REPEATS

1. Create a new file and make the artboard the dimensions of the desired repeat size (here it is 5.75" × 3.5").

Note that you can always start drawing motifs and choose a repeat/artboard size later (select *Window > Artboard*, double-click on the desired artboard, then change the width/height in the pop-up dialog). Turn on *Smart Guides* (*View > Smart Guides*). Create guides along the 4 edges of the artboard (*View > Show Rulers*; then click in the middle of the rulers and drag). Fill the center of the artboard with your design (Figure 1).

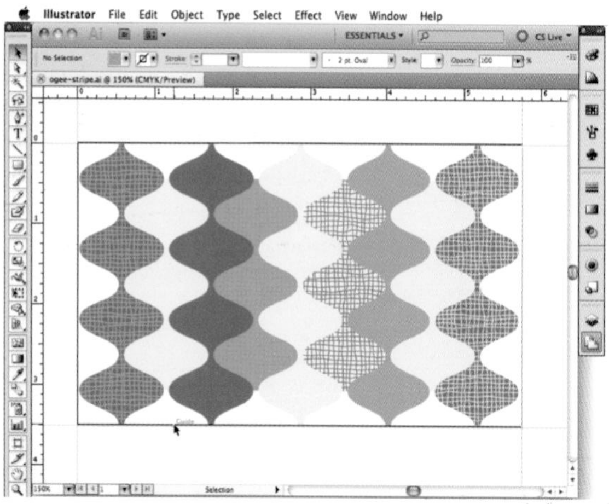

2. Add more motifs that overlap the top edge of the artboard. Here, the vertical centers of the motifs are aligned exactly with the top edge of the artboard. Group these motifs (*Object > Group*). Copy the group you just created (*Edit > Copy*) and place it along the bottom edge (*Edit > Paste*) (Figure 2).

Select the copy together with the original group, and then click the top group once more to make it a *key object*. When aligning objects, the key object will remain in place and other selected objects will align to it. Center align the 2 groups (since the top group is the key object, only the bottom group will move). Because *Smart Guides* are turned on, you will see a notation in green that the group is horizontally aligned with the bottom edge of the artboard. Edit the design as needed. Make sure that any changes made to motifs that overlap the repeat boundaries are repeated on the opposite edge.

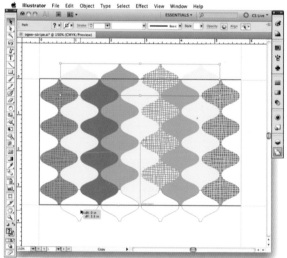

Figure 2

Figure 1

A FIELD GUIDE TO FABRIC DESIGN

3. Repeat Step 2 on the side edges (Figure 3). Because *Smart Guides* are turned on, you will see a notation in green that the group is vertically aligned with the right edge of the artboard. Also note that any motifs hitting one corner must be copied to all the other corners.

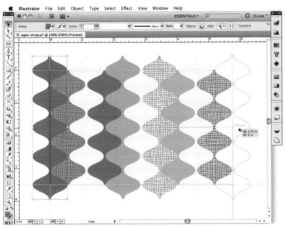

Figure 3

4. Create a rectangle the exact size of your repeat (here, 5.75" × 3.5"), with no fill or stroke weight (Figure 4). Align the rectangle with the artboard. Cut (*Edit > Cut*), and then choose *Edit > Paste in Back* (alternatively, choose *Object > Arrange > Send to Back*). The empty rectangle tells Illustrator where the repeat boundaries are. Paste another copy of the rectangle, aligned exactly with the artboard, between the empty rectangle and the motifs, and fill it with the background color, if desired. Group the background-containing box with the motifs. Select the group, drag to the *Swatches Palette*, and proof (Figure 5): Using the *Rectangle Shape Tool*, create a rectangle 2 or more times as big as your repeat in a new workspace. In the *Swatches Palette*, select the repeat pattern you just made and click on it to fill the big rectangle.

Note: Illustrator doesn't allow new patterns to be built from motifs or areas that are filled with a pattern—first you must Expand such fills, which transforms them into stand-alone objects. Before dragging your design to the Swatches palette, select the pattern-filled motifs or areas (here, the ogees filled with crosshatching) and choose Object > Expand.

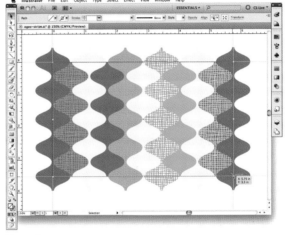

Figure 4

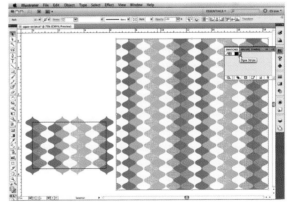

Figure 5

HALF-DROP REPEATS

1. Follow Steps 1 and 2 under Square Repeats (page 48). Your design is now in repeat along the top and bottom edges, but not yet on the sides.

2. Draw a rectangle (with no fill or stroke weight) representing the repeat boundaries as in Step 4 of Square Repeats (page 49), and center it inside the guides. Select it along with the motifs (*Select All*) and group them (*Object > Group*). Turn on *Smart Guides* (under the *View* menu), as in Figure 6. Create a horizontal center line guide by clicking on the top ruler and dragging down.

3. Create 2 copies of the selection you just made and align them as shown (Figure 7) to the right of the original (*Edit > Copy*, then *Edit > Paste*). Make sure the motifs along the bottom and top edges overlap perfectly—zoom in to check with the *Magnifying Glass* tool. The left edges of the copies should line up with the right edge of the artboard, and the bottom repeat boundary of the top right copy should align with the horizontal midline of the original. The motifs outlined in red are the duplicates here.

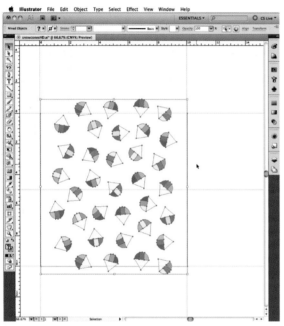

Figure 6

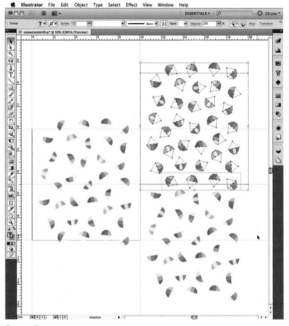

Figure 7

4. Ungroup the motifs for editing (*Select > All*, then *Object > Ungroup*). Fill in the empty vertical area between the original and the copies (Figure 8). If any previously placed motifs need editing, make sure that the other copies are edited the same way.

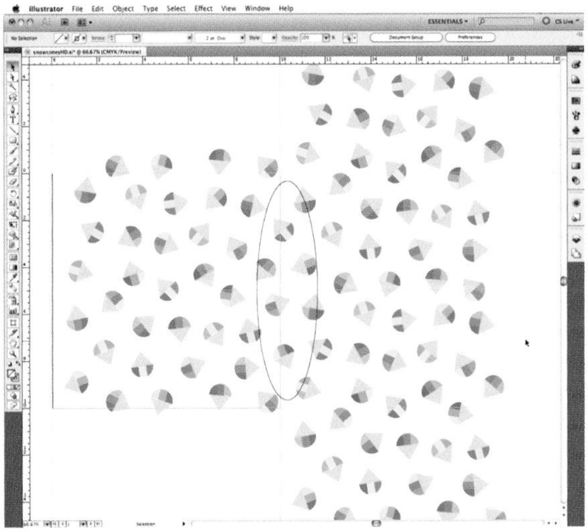

shown in Figures 9 and 10. Group these anchor boxes with the motifs that need copying (*Object > Group*, then *Edit > Copy*) and move the copy to the opposite corner. The anchor boxes will snap into place along the horizontal and vertical guides, and the motifs will be in perfect alignment.

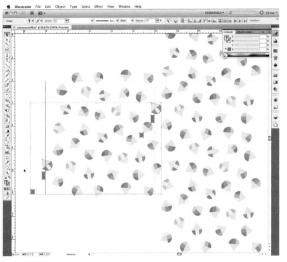

Figure 9

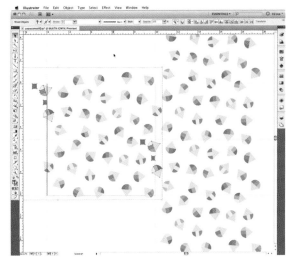

Figure 8

5. Make copies of any new motifs that intersect the right edge of the artboard/repeat boundaries as shown. If they are on the bottom half, they must be copied and placed on the top left edge; and if they're on the top half, they must be copied and placed on the lower left edge. Unless one edge of one of your motifs is aligned precisely with the repeat boundary, you can't rely on Illustrator's *Smart Guides* to snap these motifs into alignment. But here's a trick: Create 2 temporary anchor boxes—just simple squares drawn with their edges aligned to the horizontal and vertical guides, as

Figure 10

6. Ungroup and delete the anchor boxes. Delete all motifs that are not inside or overlapping the repeat boundaries. You now have a finished repeat (Figure 11).

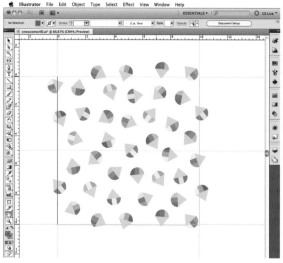

Figure 11

7. To build the repeat up to be pattern-swatch ready, you must first build the repeat up into a square repeat. Select the bounding box. Increase its width to 200%, cut it, and then *Paste in Back* or choose *Object > Arrange > Send to Back* (Figure 12). Then, select all the motifs but not the bounding box, and group them. Create 2 copies and arrange as in Step 3 (Figure 13).

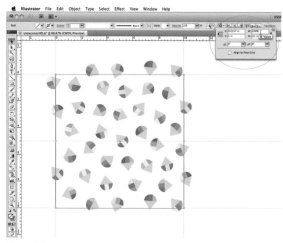

Figure 12

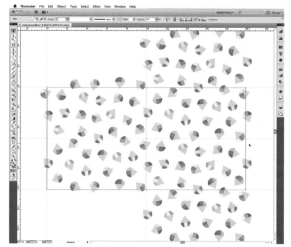

Figure 13

8. As with the block repeat, copy the bounding box and fill with background color if desired. *Group* the box containing the background with the motifs. *Select* this group together with the empty bounding box lying underneath, and then drag to the *Swatches Palette* and proof (Figure 14), as in Step 4 of Square Repeats.

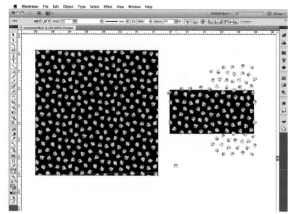

Figure 14

A FIELD GUIDE TO FABRIC DESIGN

Design Software and Tools

For designing prints on the computer, Adobe Photoshop and Illustrator are certainly the most commonly used programs. But other software and professional tools are also available. Here's a roundup of some of them.

Open-Source Software

Free, open-source software alternatives (software that is free of charge and can be used and distributed at will) to Adobe Photoshop and Illustrator are available. GIMP is a raster image editing program, and Inkscape is a vector image editing program. They function similarly to their Adobe competitors with respect to creating repeating patterns. However, you cannot work with Pantone colors in these programs. (For information about Pantone colors, see Using the Pantone Matching System, page 68.)

Specialized Textile Design Software

Though the industry is increasingly turning to Adobe Photoshop and Illustrator for printed and woven textile design (these programs are cheaper and more widely used in related industries like graphic design), more specialized software programs are available, such as a design suite produced by NedGraphics (nedgraphics.com), that make repeat setup and coloring a snap when designing pattern repeats. They're usually not affordable for the individual designer, but still, you can dream. Fashion Toolbox (fashiontoolbox.com) is an affordable, PC-compatible fashion design suite with lots of similar features.

Artlandia (artlandia.com) produces affordable plug-ins for Photoshop and Illustrator called SymmetryShop and

SymmetryWorks, respectively. These programs build dozens of pattern and repeat types from editable "seed" motifs at the touch of a button directly onto the screen; there is no need to create individual pattern swatches and proof the patterns by drawing and filling new shapes. When editing the seed motifs of a repeat, all other instances of that motif are instantly updated. Their LivePresets plug-in for Illustrator allows the user to create "live" (editable) pattern swatches. Link the swatches to digitally draped sewn products, and the rendering updates before your eyes as you edit the pattern.

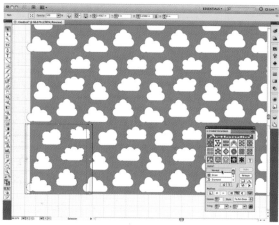

Artlandia SymmetryShop screenshot

Professional Tools

Drawing tablets. Designers and artists of all kinds *adore* their drawing tablets. These tablets replace or supplement a mouse with a penlike device and drawing surface, making drawing and tracing on the computer screen much more natural. Wacom (wacom.com) is the biggest and best-known manufacturer of drawing tablets. At this writing, touch-screen technology is becoming more affordable and widely available, which will allow designers to draw directly onto the screen. This technology will likely replace drawing tablets in the years to come.

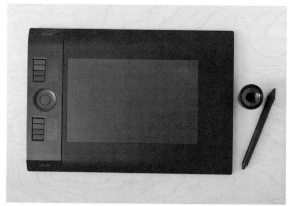

Wacom drawing tablet

A FIELD GUIDE TO FABRIC DESIGN

Proofing Repeats: Why and How

It's vital to *proof* (or *render* or *tile*) your pattern so you can see how it looks in repeat. This is a snap in Illustrator and Photoshop; simply draw a large rectangle (in Illustrator) or open a new file (in Photoshop) that is several times the size of your repeat and fill it using the pattern swatch you created at the end of the Designing Repeats by Computer tutorials earlier in this chapter. It also helps to print your design out on paper and tape the tiled pieces together on your design wall so that you can see if you like how it flows. Proofing will help identify misalignments along the repeat edges. To render a repeat for proofing by hand, simply place the original design beneath a large sheet of tracing paper, trace, then move the original over one repeat (placed according to the chosen repeat type, see page 20), and trace again.

Identifying Problems

Unless you are creating a set pattern, people should have to work a little to find your repeat. (Of course, like all things in art and design, this is subject to taste.) The pattern should flow; the eye should move around and not immediately notice how certain motifs line up over the length of the fabric. *Unintentional* interruptions to the flow are called *tracking* or *striping*.

Tracking happens when some design parameter—usually direction, shape, color, or scale of a motif—is not in balance with the rest of the design, revealing the repeat in an unpleasant manner. For instance, in a tossed pattern, two motifs might point in the same direction, pulling the eye diagonally when it shouldn't be going in any one direction at all. As another example, it would be a big challenge to put a baguette in a four-way French café–themed print among

coffee cups, a Brie wheel, and croissants without its oblong shape creating unintentional stripes.

Color is a big culprit in tracking. In this floral photo collage design, you can clearly see the tracking issue due to groups of white-colored roses standing out from the pinkish and greenish roses.

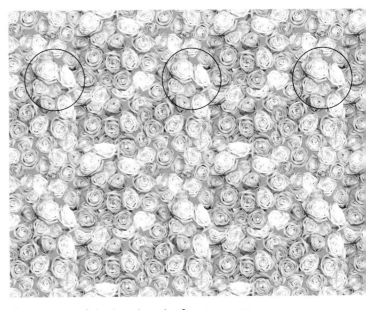

If the cause of the break in the flow is negative space—space not filled in with the design—it is called an *alleyway*. Alleyways occur when some empty areas of the repeat are too big compared with others, or when these areas form distinct, directional shapes.

Stepping back or zooming out can help identify problems you might not have noticed up close. Leaving the design for a while and coming back to it with fresh eyes is also very helpful. And of course it's always good to have a partner take a look; maybe he or she can point out problems you didn't notice.

Adobe Illustrator and my iMac.
—DENYSE SCHMIDT

Well it's certainly easier with a computer, but since I'm a painter as well, I could do it by hand if I needed to! —MELISSA AVERINOS

I always want my designs to have a hand-drawn feeling. It gives them a warmth and quirkiness that is very appealing to me. So, without a doubt, my favorite tool is my Wacom drawing tablet. It allows me to create truly hand-drawn designs directly on the computer, which keeps my artistic process very fast and simple without sacrificing that unique hand-drawn quality. —JASONDA DESMOND

Mechanical pencil and graphed fade-out vellum, without a doubt. A giant eraser for all of those mistakes that I never ever make. —TULA PINK

Well I've done it completely by hand with paints and pens and copiers and overlays with marker. Now I do the initial designs and layouts by hand, and my assistant Molly creates the digital art in the computer and I color it there. We've had to make that giant leap because of the demands on the design and the way the prints are used not only for fabric but other products. So this is a hard question, because I could still go back and do it the old-fashioned way. Favorite tools: Maybe my reading glasses? Or an X-Acto knife! —AMY BUTLER

Solving Problems

Once you've identified these tracking and alleyway problems, how do you fix them? There's no one answer, but here are a few fixes to try.

- Change the repeat from a block to a half-drop.
- Remove, rotate, or recolor the offending motif(s).
- Think big. Bigger repeat sizes mean that repeating elements are farther apart and there is more to distract the eye in between. To fix tracking issues when working with a smaller repeat, try tiling the original repeat one across and one over to make a 2 × 2 set and editing elements within this new, quadruple-sized repeat.

Spot Repeats

Spot repeats are the designer's secret weapon for balancing nondirectional prints, and they can work for other directionalities too. It's a bit like playing Sudoku with motifs (only this is much easier). Divide a square repeat unit into a grid, from 3 × 3 on up. Place motifs so that each one gets its row and column to itself, and vary each motif's rotation if creating a tossed design. Once these units are in repeat, there might be a noticeable diagonal flow, which you may or may not like. Furthermore, some "solutions" to the puzzle will result in tracking or alleyways, so you may have to experiment with different arrangements.

Using the spot repeat concept, you can also create continuous patterns. First, place major motifs such as showy flowers in the grid; then interconnect them with elements like stems or vines.

SPOT REPEAT GRIDS

3- THROUGH 8-SPOT GRIDS

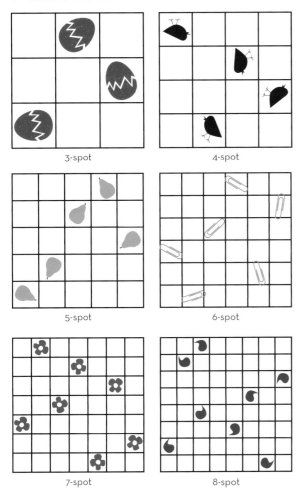

3-spot

4-spot

5-spot

6-spot

7-spot

8-spot

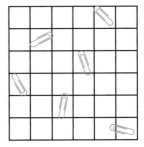

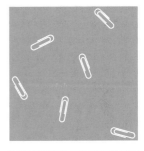

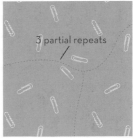

3 partial repeats

Paper clip 6-spot design, recolored and put in to repeat (3 partial repeats shown in bottom illustration)

Ideas for Adding Interest

Here's a list of things to try when you're playing with designs or are stuck for ideas on how to make a design work:

- Use a different repeat type (for example, change a block repeat to a half-drop).

- Vary the scale of the motifs within the design.

- Add different motifs, or edit down to fewer motifs. (Sometimes more is more; sometimes less is more!)

- Fill solid areas or backgrounds with simple patterns.

- Play with silhouettes and outlines of motifs.

- Start over and render motifs in different media (for example, change from a computer-drawn design and draw it by hand instead).

Know Your Color

People are drawn in by color; they are soothed or energized by it. It can cause a rush of nostalgia or propel you forward with its freshness and originality. The colors we choose to wear and to surround ourselves with at home say so much about who we are. Color attracts people to your fabric as much as—sometimes more than—any other aspect of its design. It can be intimidating to work with, but through a combination of technical knowledge and play, many designers find it to be the most satisfying aspect of fabric design. In this chapter, you'll learn about developing harmonious color schemes and applying them to your designs in a way that ensures that the final print matches your original vision.

Masters at Work

Perhaps the ultimate examples of effective, professional use of color are fabrics designed by the Kaffe Fassett collective, which includes Fassett, desiger/studio manager Brandon Mably, and designer Philip Jacobs. They are masters of color. Their motifs are imaginative and beautiful, but these aspects are all vehicles for their unique expression of color. Though each designer releases new collections regularly, each flows into the larger body of work rather than standing as isolated statements. Colorways include pastel, earthy brown, hot colors, cool colors, and vibrant black, each totally changing the mood of—and potential audience for—the design. To which do you respond the most?

English Rose by Philip Jacobs for Westminster Fabrics

Developing Effective Color Palettes and Schemes

Do you lack confidence when it comes to combining colors? Maybe you have a favorite color and a few favorite color pairings, but coming up with schemes of three or more colors makes you freeze up. It's a common problem, but it's easily remedied by three methods: borrowing color ideas, using color theory, and playing with color. These are not mutually exclusive, but all will help you gain confidence in your ability to develop beautiful, harmonious palettes.

Borrowing Color from Source Material

The easiest route to an effective color palette is to take it from another source. Fortunately, this is perfectly legal; colors and color combinations are not subject to copyright. The same handful of colors tends to look completely new in the hands of each designer and when applied in different proportions to different designs, so the chances of appearing derivative are slim. However, I wouldn't recommend using another artist's (especially another fabric designer's) color palettes "verbatim." Instead, use a subset, which you can edit or expand to help express your unique ideas. Source material for a color palette can be anything—a photograph, works of art, product packaging, vintage textiles, paint samples from home improvement stores, or a painting, to name a few. Consider taking a trip to the local home improvement store to collect paint chips or other color samples.

Note:

In some instances color has been trademarked. For the difference between copyright and trademark, go to www.uspto.gov/patents < General Information Concerning Patents [HTML] > What Are Patents, Trademarks, Servicemarks, and Copyrights?

For general information on copyright, see Copyright Primer (page 30).

You can always rely on source material you "borrow" from nature, such as leaves, a bird's feathers, or a landscape, for harmonious color palettes. I recommend keeping a color journal—a central place to gather and store clippings of colors and color combinations that inspire you.

You can scan source materials to extract their colors for use directly in your designs or to manipulate into new palettes. If you prefer manual methods, you can refer to the source material as you mix up paints or pull prepared color swatches from a color library. We'll discuss these manual and digital methods in the following pages.

Often, the colors pulled from source material are insufficient for your needs. A basic understanding of color theory can help you expand or adjust the palette to suit your design.

Schemes, Palettes, and Colorways

The terms *color scheme*, *color palette*, and *colorway* are often used interchangeably, but in this book each has its own definition.

Color Scheme: A group of colors built on the harmonic relationships on the color wheel.

Color Palette: A group of colors assembled without the intentional use of these harmonic relationships.

Colorway: Once color schemes or palettes are applied to a textile, the differently colored versions of the same design are referred to as colorways. A group of different prints with a cohesive color palette is also called a colorway, or sometimes a *color story*, because it helps to express the designer's ideas. (I use the term *color story* for this latter application.) Colorways are discussed further in Colorways and Collections (page 80).

61

Using Color Theory

Though color theory is often perceived as dry and intimidating, just a few basics will give you access to a limitless supply of harmonious color palettes. The more well versed you are in color theory, the more power you have to tell the story you want to tell with your designs. Color theory also offers a structured approach to color, which helps fight the dreaded option paralysis (see Developing Your Design Style, page 26).

THE COLOR WHEEL

You have probably encountered the color wheel before. The wheel features twelve pure colors, called *hues*. The *primary colors*—red, blue, and yellow—are arranged equidistant from one another. The spaces between them are filled with *secondary colors* (green, orange, and violet, the results of mixing equal portions of two primary colors) and sometimes with tertiary colors as well. Tertiary colors result from mixing equal proportions of a primary color and a secondary color. The six basic tertiary colors are yellow-orange, red-orange, red-violet, blue-violet, blue-green, and yellow-green.

To build your first color schemes using the color wheel, I recommend using good old-fashioned paint. Watercolors, acrylics, or gouache (an opaque watercolor) will do. Of course, computers make this process a snap, and you'll learn later in the chapter how to build harmonious color schemes digitally. But for understanding the basics, paint is ideal.

The twelve pure colors shown in the basic color wheel are referred to as *hues*. Altering these hues by adding white, black, or gray produces *tints*, *shades*, and *tones*, respectively. Tints are commonly referred to as pastels.

Value refers to the darkness or lightness of a hue. Adding white or black gives a hue a lighter or darker value, respectively.

Saturation or *chroma* refers to the purity and intensity of a hue. Adding white, black, or gray decreases the chroma.

Temperature refers to warm and cool colors. Reds, oranges, and yellows are considered the warm side of the color wheel; greens, blues, and violets are the cool side.

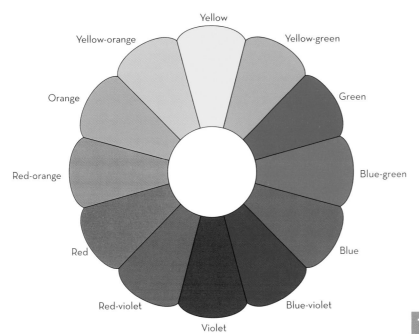

Yellow

Yellow-orange   Yellow-green

Orange   Green

Red-orange   Blue-green

Red   Blue

Red-violet   Blue-violet

Violet

Basic color wheel

Pure hues

Tints

Tones

Shades

Color wheel showing pure hues, tints, shades, and tones

TIP

You may encounter different types of color wheels based on different primary colors (for example: cyan, magenta, and yellow) or on fewer or more colors, but similar principles and rules underlie them all.

Basic Color Schemes

Harmonious color schemes are created by combining hues that lie in a logical relationship to one another on the color wheel. Examples of some basic schemes are illustrated on these pages.

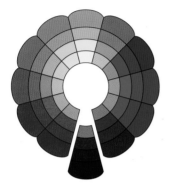

Monochromatic: Tints, shades, and tones of a single hue such as violet

Complement: Two hues such as yellow-green and red-violet that lie across from each other on the color wheel. In juxtaposition, these colors make each other appear brighter, and the boundaries where they meet appear to vibrate.

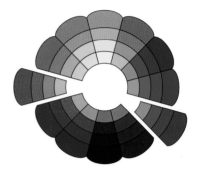

Near Complement: One hue in combination with the neighbor of its complement, such as blue with red-orange

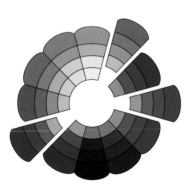

Split Complement: One hue in combination with the hues on either side of its complement, such as red with yellow-green and blue-green

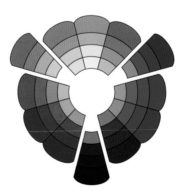

Triad: A combination of three hues spaced evenly on the color wheel; for example, green, violet, and orange. This is a popular choice for multicolored fabrics.

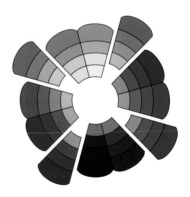

Tetrad: A combination of four hues spaced evenly on the color wheel; for example, blue, red-violet, orange, and yellow-green.

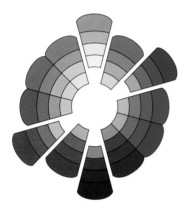

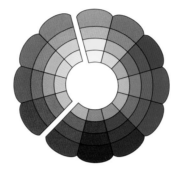

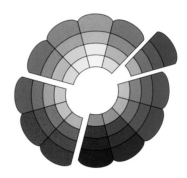

Rectangular Tetrad: A pair of complements together with the hues two spots over, such as yellow and violet with red and green.

Analogous: Three or more hues that are adjacent on the color wheel, such as yellow-orange, orange, red-orange, and red

Analogous Complement: Three analogous hues together with the complement of the center hue, such as red-violet, red, and red-orange with green

DESIGNER TIP: NEUTRALS

Though grays and browns are called neutrals, they do not necessarily harmonize with every color palette because they often contain undertones of other colors. The best way to achieve a harmonious gray is to mix a speck of your scheme's dominant color with a true gray (a gray made only with black and white). For a harmonious brown, mix together two complementary colors used in your scheme in equal proportions. Add white or black to the gray or brown to lighten or darken it.

Some of the color combinations suggested by these basic schemes might not appeal to you. (Blue and orange? Purple, orange, and green? Ewww!) But don't let that stop you from using the real power of the color wheel. Take these schemes as foundations; the magic happens when you start mixing the colors in the scheme together in various proportions. Try choosing one color from the basic scheme as a dominant or main color, and add just a tiny speck to each of the other colors in the scheme. The result is a new palette of toned-down, complex, and always harmonious colors. You can further extend the scheme by adding tints, shades, and tones of the basic hues and the mixtures thereof.

Palette Play

Even if you choose to avoid color theory, you can simply play with color to find palettes that speak to you. Become a color collector and create a home-made color swatch library. Save scraps of solid fabric whenever you can. Paint chips, yarns, and anything else with a solid color are nice too, but fabric is ideal.

Amassing a color swatch collection can yield several advantages. Your color library will become a great source of inspiration (and will look pretty on display!). Fabric swatches also give you a closer approximation of how colors will look when they are printed onto fabric than do computer screen or paint colors. Your swatches will also come in handy if you are working with a fabric manu-facturer and need to provide physical samples of your colors.

You can use source material (see Borrowing Color from Source Material, page 60) as a jumping-off point for choosing swatches rather than trying to match your source's colors exactly. For example, I wasn't completely satisfied with the digital color palette I extracted from this photo of blueberries, so I pulled fabric swatches that better represented my idea of the colors and extended the palette with a couple of complementary accents and neutrals.

Homemade color swatch library

Working with Digital Color

Many modern fabric designers never touch paint; all their color work is done via the computer. Whether you are planning to incor-porate computers into your design work or use them as your only design tool, here is a primer that will help you navigate the com-plex world of digital color and its relationship to fabric printing.

In a nutshell, digital color has limited usefulness in the fabric design process, and no matter which design or printing method you're using, the best practice is to refer to phys-ical color swatches for your color information. You'll learn more about why and how to use them in this section.

Color Models

You will encounter several different *color models* (sometimes called *color spaces*) when designing on the computer. These are theoretical models that quantitatively define colors based on different components. Here are the most commonly used color models explained in layman's terms.

RGB: This is a model based on emitted light in the primary colors of red (R), green (G), and blue (B). Colored light acts differently than paint or ink. Red, green, and blue light combined in equal proportions makes white; while an equal mixture of red, green, and blue pigments creates black. Computer screens, TVs, and other electronic devices use the RGB model. Hex color codes are RGB colors in a code that is readable by web browsers. There are no absolute standards for these colors; the model merely tells the device how to make the colors, but they end up looking a bit different on every screen.

CMYK: Also known as process color, this model is based on the application of mixtures of inks—cyan (C), magenta (M), yellow (Y), and black (K)—to a white surface. It also refers to the printing process that uses this model. Tiny dots of each color are laid on the paper in various proportions, and the eye reads them as solid colors. You can work with CMYK colors on a computer, but what you see are approximations of CMYK colors rendered via RGB.

HSV, HSL, and HSB: These models define colors by their relative hue (H), saturation (S), and value (V) or lightness (L) or brightness (B). They are derived from the RGB model but based on more familiar and intuitive color-mixing concepts.

Lab, also known as L*,a*,b* and **CIELAB:** These models are designed to approximate all colors perceptible to the human eye. They are based on lightness (L) and on two color-opponent dimensions (red-green and yellow-blue), labeled *a* and *b* respectively.

DESIGNER TIP *In Adobe Photoshop, the Color Picker allows you to supply codes for HSB, RGB, CMYK, Lab, and hex colors. In Adobe Illustrator, the Swatch Options dialog does the same thing. (Colors untranslatable from one model to another will be indicated as "out of gamut.") More budget-conscious software (such as Photoshop Elements) and free, open-source image editing programs (such as GIMP) typically support only HSB, RGB, and hex colors.*

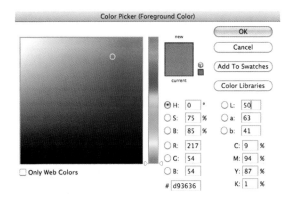

The range of colors that is possible to achieve given the ingredients of the model is called its *gamut*, and it is different for each model. Remember that each model is theoretical, though. As you might imagine, real life is less perfect. Any given computer monitor or printer has its own variables, which limit and alter the input of the color model. The achievable output of a given device, given a certain color model as input, is also called a gamut.

The choice of color model you work with is really only a concern if you are printing digitally (see Digital Printing, page 134). Ask your print bureau (digital printing service) which color model they recommend—RGB, CMYK, or Lab—for preparing your file. You can use a different model from the one they recommend, but the bureau's printer software will convert your image to that recommended model before printing, and a color shift might occur as a result.

Most digital printing bureaus supply color charts that show how a set of colors looks printed by their printers onto their fabric. You will read more about these charts and how to use them in Color in Digital Printing (page 138). The colors in these charts might be rendered from any of the models we've discussed. You input the code of your chosen color from the chart into the color picker in your image editing program.

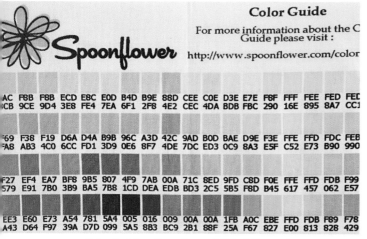

Color chart from Spoonflower digital printing service

If you are printing with DIY methods such as block printing or screen printing, or you are licensing your designs for volume printing, your choice of color model is not crucial. These printing methods all use *spot colors*—inks/dyes that are premixed, one for each color in the print, before applying them to the base cloth. Spot colors are either mixed by eye with use of the color wheel, just like paints, or with the use of a standard system, such as the Pantone Matching System (see Using the Pantone Matching System, at right, for more on Pantone). The Pantone Matching System includes formulas for mixing inks. This not only takes away guesswork but also makes it easier to achieve color consistency over long or multiple print runs. Spot color systems also have their own gamuts, and there is no one-to-one correspondence with any of the color models previously discussed.

Color Standards

When designing on the computer for any print method, think of the colors you see on your screen as placeholders only; the real color information has to come from a physical reference, or *standard*. The colors on your digital print bureau's color chart serve as standards. Your homemade swatch library can be a standard, too; you can send swatches to a manufacturer or mill to communicate the exact colors you want, or use them as references for mixing block-printing or screen-printing inks by eye. If you have access to Pantone Matching System swatches—a widely used color standards system—you can use them in conjunction with or in place of your homemade swatch library. Only the more expensive Pantone sets feature large, detachable, mix-and-match swatches. The more affordable sets are not as conducive to developing schemes and palettes via color play.

DESIGNER TIP

Many designers who license their work to fabric manufacturers or agents submit their work on paper, and their color printouts or painted swatches serve as standards. Because fabric has a different texture, opacity, and absorption than paper, these paper standards are not ideal for designs to be printed on fabric, but they usually do the job.

USING THE PANTONE MATCHING SYSTEM

The Pantone Matching System (PMS) is a spot-color standards system that is widely used throughout the graphics and textile industries. It is a color space like those discussed under Color Models (page 67) with its own gamut, but it is proprietary to the company. The idea behind the Pantone Matching System, which is based on formulas for mixing inks and dyes, is to allow everyone in the chain of design and production to match specific colors among different

A FIELD GUIDE TO FABRIC DESIGN

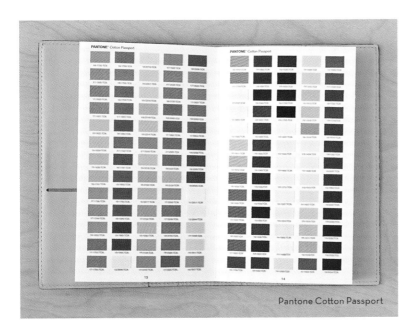

Pantone Cotton Passport

devices, equipment, and substrates. Since most manufacturers and mills also use this system, you can simply provide the color numbers you are using rather than sending physical swatches. (If they don't use the system, you can purchase individual chips or swatches from Pantone to send, rather than going through the trouble of painting or printing your own or assembling your own fabric swatches, in which case you might not be able to find a specific color.)

The basic Pantone Formula Guide paper fans, which provide formulas for mixing inks (including screen-printing inks), retail at a little over $100 at this writing. Pantone's Fashion + Home system offers Pantone colors as a library of cotton swatches in various sizes and configurations. It's the ideal standard to use in fabric design, but it's considerably more expensive. Most designers find that the paper fans serve their needs adequately.

Pantone has an ever-expanding range of products that can be very confusing to the uninitiated. Whether you're hand printing or licensing your designs for commercial printing, the paper Formula Guide (uncoated) is a great all-purpose choice. The paper Fashion + Home Color Guide provides a better representation of how the colors translate to fabric, but the cotton products, of course, are the ideal. Of all the cotton products, the Cotton Passport is the least expensive, but the swatches are tiny and cannot be removed from the pages.

No matter which Pantone system products you use, you can cross-reference the color numbers for free on their website (see Resources, page 158).

Adobe Photoshop and Illustrator users can also work on-screen with representations of Pantone colors. Several Pantone digital swatch libraries come packaged with these design programs. Illustrator's Color Guide (see it in action in the Applying Color Schemes in Illustrator tutorial, page 72) works with these libraries, generating harmonious schemes from single Pantone colors.

Pantone has its own free software, myPantone (www.pantone.com/pages/MYP_myPantone/mypantone.aspx), for generating schemes and sharing them online; but the digital color swatch libraries, such as the Fashion + Home colors, that drive the program cost $10–$20 each.

Digital Color Palette Software and Resources

These stand-alone software programs, online tools, and blogs allow you to borrow or build beautiful, harmonious color schemes easily.

Kuler

kuler.adobe.com

Adobe's free online application brings color inspiration together with social networking. Users create and share color schemes generated from digital photos or the color wheel, and explore and save others' palettes. Supports HSV, RGB/hex, CMYK, and Lab models. Adobe CS4 and up have built-in Kuler interactivity. Palettes are limited to five colors.

ColourLovers

colourlovers.com

This is a color scheme creation and sharing community site that is free to join and use. Their advanced color palette generation tool, COPASO, supports RGB, HSV, and CMYK models and lets you build schemes based on five different harmonic relationships (complementary, triadic, and so on). Schemes are limited to five colors, though. ColourLovers also has a cool pattern generation and coloring feature and an informative and inspirational blog. They're partnered with digital textile printing bureau Spoonflower (see Resources, page 158), so you can buy fabric printed with your design.

ColorSchemer Studio

colorschemer.com

This paid software (Mac and PC available) builds harmonious color schemes from single colors or from scratch. It can also pull color from digital images. If you are accustomed to mixing paint, this is a great tool. You tell it which colors to mix and how many intermediary mixtures you want, and it does the work for you. Schemes can be imported and exported in a variety of formats. Supports CMYK, RGB/hex, and HSB models.

Blogs

KRISTINA KLARIN

kristinaklarin.blogspot.com

On this blog, designer Kristina Klarin paints up color palettes from inspirational images.

COLOR COLLECTIVE

color-collective.blogspot.com

Five-color palettes pulled from the work of various designers, artists, and photographers are shown in this blog.

WEAR PALETTES

blog.wearpalettes.com

Five-color palettes pulled from everyday and celebrity fashions are featured here.

Applying Color

Now that you have the ability to work up beautiful color palettes and schemes in a variety of ways, it's time to apply the colors to your designs.

Hand Painting Designs

Hand painting your design is straightforward. Whether you use paint, ink, marker, or another medium, transfer your hand-drawn design to the appropriate substrate, and then start painting. You can also print outlines from a digitally created design onto paper (or onto the sturdier paint-ready substrate, if your printer is able to handle it).

This process can be labor-intensive, especially if you are testing various color palettes. To make this job easier, start by coloring a *croquis*, which is a snippet or a quick and sketchy mock-up of a design idea. Designers usually use croquis in the initial stages to work out motifs and colors before the design is put into repeat. Some designers work exclusively with croquis and leave the creation of repeats to other professionals. Of course, if you are printing with a DIY method or sending your designs to a digital print bureau, you don't have this luxury. But you can still use croquis to work out your color palettes.

The paint of choice for hand coloring designs is gouache, which is a type of pigment paint that is thinned and cleaned up with water but dries opaque. Compared with other types of paint, the matte surface of dried gouache is most like that of fabric.

Some professional designers submit hand-painted designs (in repeat or croquis form) to fabric companies and other agents, though many professionals I spoke to said that hand painting repeats is fast becoming a lost art. Swatches of the colors in the design are also painted adjacent to the design for reference. If you are hand-painting a design for digital printing, you would need to edit the design in a raster editing program like Adobe Photoshop to repair the seams between the repeats before uploading your design.

Using Swatches

You can also use physical swatches as a starting point for colors to apply to a design. If you are hand painting a design or hand mixing your block-printing or screen-printing inks, you can simply use the swatches for reference and mix colors in an attempt to match them. The swatches can also be used to choose colors from a digital print bureau's color chart. If you are creating designs on the computer to send off to a manufacturer, you can scan the swatches, extract the colors, and apply them according to the tutorials that follow.

You can also use inexpensive smartphone applications (such as colorID by Winfield & Co. LLC for the iPhone) to photograph swatches. The app tells you the color's code for RGB/hex, CMYK, and other models. If you don't have this device, simply choosing colors on-screen that approximate your swatch colors is okay. As discussed earlier, screen colors are more or less meaningless; the physical standard is what is used for color information.

Beware the White Background!

White-background print stack

I am a sucker for prints on white backgrounds, especially novelties. While the rest of my stash gets used and replenished, though, this part remains relatively static. Why? In my experience, their attractiveness is out of proportion with their usefulness. They show dirt, and the high contrast means trouble getting along with other fabrics. If you do choose a white background for a design, do so mindfully. When putting together collections, make sure high-contrast prints are balanced with other lower-contrast ones. DIY printing is usually and most easily done on a white or natural fabric (I prefer natural of course), but I discuss in the hand-printing tutorials (see Step-by-Step Hand Printing, page 110) how you can print with pigments on any color background. With other methods (digital, mass production) you have the choice of background color.

APPLYING COLOR SCHEMES IN ILLUSTRATOR

With version CS3, Illustrator introduced two powerful color tools: the Color Guide and Live Color (renamed Recolor Artwork in later versions). The Color Guide allows the user to generate an infinite variety of harmonious color wheel–based schemes automatically from a color of choice. It's like the digital color tools (see Digital Color Palette Software and Resources, page 70), but without limits on the number of colors. The Live Color / Recolor Artwork tool allows the user to quickly replace one color scheme with another.

1. After opening or creating your design, open a swatch library. Open the *Swatches* panel (*Window > Swatches*). Click on its *Options* menu (arrow + list icon in the top right corner), and then choose *Open Swatch Library* from the menu. From there, you can choose from several libraries that come packaged with Illustrator or choose *Other Library* (Figure 1). This will allow you to find libraries that you saved as .ase files (meaning Adobe Swatch Exchange) through any of the digital color tools listed (see Digital Color Palette Software and Resources, page 70). Here, I have preloaded several 5-color palettes and schemes drawn from various online sources.

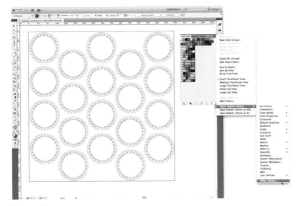

Figure 1

2. Select the palette you wish to work with by clicking on the folder icon next to the swatches (Figure 2).

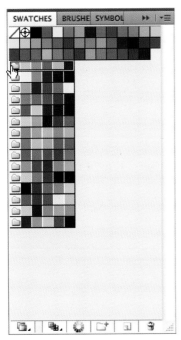

Figure 2

3. Open the *Color Guide* (*Window > Color Guide*) to view the selected swatch library. Shades and tints of the original colors are displayed in addition to the original swatches. Via the *Options* menu situated in the upper right corner of the *Color Guide*, you can also choose to display other variations of the original swatches—such as *Warm/Cool* and *Vivid/Muted*—and to display more or fewer variants (Figure 3). You can also click on all or some of the variants to select them, and then save them as swatches from the *Options* menu. They will then appear back in the *Swatches* panel.

Figure 3

4. Working from the expanded library of harmonious color swatches, start choosing colors as fill and stroke colors for your motifs. Here, the design is shown after I chose the initial colors (Figure 4).

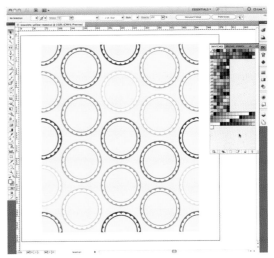

Figure 4

Using the Recolor Artwork Tool in Illustrator

- With the *Selection Arrow* tool, select all objects to be recolored. Open the *Recolor Artwork* panel (*Edit > Edit Colors > Recolor Artwork*) (Figure 1). You can also recolor a pattern fill inside an object if the object is selected. The *Recolor Artwork* panel provides access to the *Color Picker*, which allows you to select a current color and then input desired color number codes for a new color (say, from a digital printing bureau's color chart, or from your Pantone book of choice).

the color wheel changes the saturation of the wheel as a whole for a new set of options.

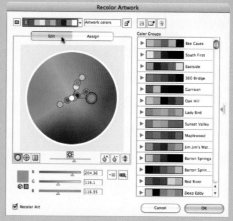

Figure 2: Smooth color wheel

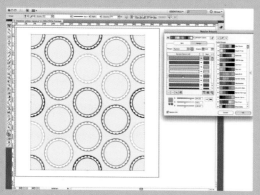

Figure 1

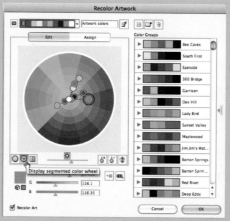

Figure 3: Segmented color wheel

- Choose the *Edit* button in the *Recolor Artwork* panel. You'll see a color wheel, which you can choose to display as smooth (Figure 2, with the hues gradually blended together) or segmented (Figure 3, like the familiar color wheel presented earlier in the chapter). Current colors used in the artwork are circled. Choose the lower right *Link Harmony Colors* button to preserve the relationship between the colors, if desired. This is helpful for preserving a color scheme type (e.g., a triadic or split complementary scheme) while changing the hues' values or the hues themselves. Drag one of the circles toward or away from the center (Figures 4, 5, and 6) to change to tints or shades of the same colors. You can also rotate around the wheel for a new set of hues that preserves the relationship between the original colors. The slider below

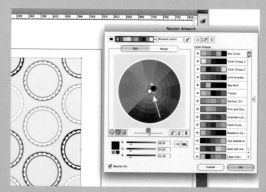

Figure 4: Design is recolored by linking harmony colors and pushing them toward the center of the wheel, resulting in lighter values.

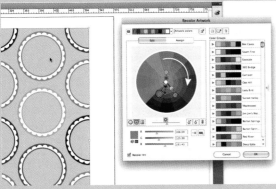

Figure 5: The design is recolored by linking harmony colors and rotating the colors around the wheel a few spaces over, but keeping the same values as the original colors.

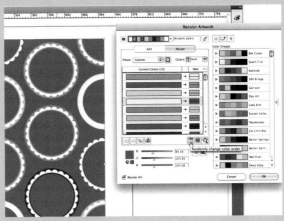

Figure 7

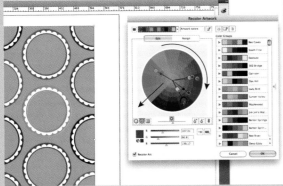

Figure 6: The design is recolored by linking harmony colors, rotating the colors around the wheel, and pulling them out toward the darker values.

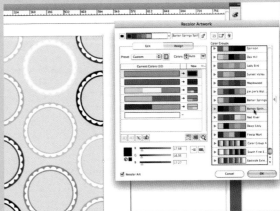

Figure 8

- Clicking the *Assign* button in the *Recolor Artwork* panel opens up options for recoloring. Current artwork colors are shown in the left-hand column, and new colors are shown to their right. Drag the colors in the *New* column to swap them with another current color. Click the buttons below the *New* column to randomly rearrange the colors or randomly change their saturation and brightness (Figure 7).

- You can also assign colors from a previously saved swatch group. Click the *Assign* button, if you haven't already. The list of saved swatch groups is in the right-hand column. If you don't see it, click the arrow on the right side of the panel to expand the window. Click on a new

swatch group. Note that if more colors are in the original artwork than in the new palette, two or more original colors will be mapped to one new color (Figure 8). From there, the newly assigned colors can be switched around or edited in a myriad of ways—just start playing with the numerous options. Edited swatch groups can be saved anew by clicking on the folder icon at the top of the panel.

DESIGNER TIP *With Illustrator's Recolor Artwork function, auditioning new colorways is amazingly fast and easy. When you hit upon a colorway you like, be sure to save the design as a new file, or else you might not be able to re-create the colors later!*

APPLYING COLOR SCHEMES IN PHOTOSHOP

Though Photoshop is not as feature-rich as Illustrator in regard to color, applying color in Photoshop to line art is just as straightforward.

1. Open your design. Here, I am using un-anti-aliased line art (drawn by my husband) already in repeat, scanned and prepared according to the instructions in Scanning Line Art for Fabric Design (page 40).

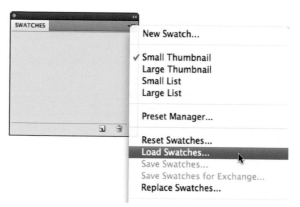

Load swatches

Uncolored design

2. Open the *Swatches* panel. You can't organize different swatch groups in folders as you can in Illustrator, so it's best to work with one group at a time. Empty out the default swatches by holding down the *Option* key as you click on each swatch. The cursor will turn into scissors. Then, use the *Color Picker* to input color values from a digital color blanket, Pantone book, or other standards, and save each color by clicking *Add to Swatches*.

Note:

Alternatively, import saved swatch groups (.ase files) from Illustrator or any of the free sources (see Digital Color Palette Software and Resources sidebar, page 70) by choosing Load Swatches *from the* Swatch Palette's Options *menu.*

3. Create a layer underneath the motifs layer (*Layer > New Layer*) and fill it with a background color or a simple pattern.

4. Return to the layer containing your motifs, and use the *Paint Bucket* tool. If you'd like to change the outline colors all at once, uncheck the *Contiguous* option in the top toolbar, pick the new color from the *Swatch Palette*, and click on any of the outlines. To change each motif's outline individually, check the *Contiguous* option, pick a new color from the *Swatch Palette*, and then click on the outline you wish to color.

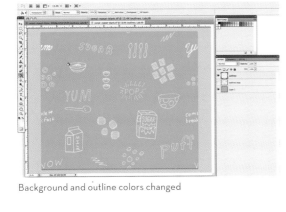

Background and outline colors changed

5. To fill in the motifs, click to check the *Contiguous* option if it is not already checked. Fill in blank areas and outlines as desired. You may decide to fill in a motif with the same color as its outline; if so, those colors will form one solid area and you won't be able to change the outline color anymore. Saving a copy of the layer with the original motifs will provide a backup should you wish to switch back to the outlines. *Hint:* Holding down the *Option* key turns the *Paint Bucket* tool into the *Eyedropper*. If you have lots of areas to color, as I do here, this shortcut comes in handy.

Finally, don't forget to color both portions of a motif that is split in two by the repeat boundaries.

Here is the finished design. To create a new colorway, use the *Magic Wand* tool with *Contiguous* checked to select all areas of a single color in the design, and then use the *Paint Bucket* to fill in all these areas at once with the new color.

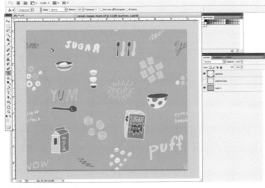

Finished, colored design

Coloring Anti-Aliased Line Art

To preserve the smooth edges of anti-aliased artwork as you color, first select the motif layer or layers in the *Layers Palette*. Click the little checkerboard icon as shown to lock the transparency. Then you can color the outlines with the *Paint Bucket* as in Steps 4 and 5 (at left). To color inside the lines, create a new layer underneath the motifs, and working on that new layer, use the *Paintbrush* tool to color in. To recolor, lock the transparency of this layer, and drop in colors the easy way with the *Paint Bucket*.

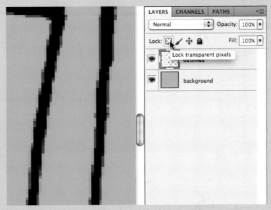

Lock transparency.

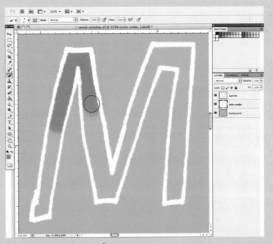

Painting under the motifs

KNOW YOUR COLOR

Color is what my brand is all about, so I never reuse palettes from one fabric collection to the next. Figuring out the new color palette is one of my favorite parts of the design process! For each year I create new palettes for the fabrics and other products I'm working on. Certainly some colors make repeat appearances, but it's not intentional. My current color palette consists of 182 colors—I need to get immersed in all the colors before I settle on the palettes for specific collections. —AMY BUTLER

Yes, I like to use a core set of colors and springboard off that in one direction or another, depending on the season. I've been consistent with my color preferences for many years; I'm happy to stay within the confines of certain basics that I always feel work well for me and with each other. This is not unlike most apparel brands; there is typically a core set (this is "our" navy, this is "our" red) and all the "fashion colors" vary from season to season. It helps to unify the brand and keeps things flowing from one collection to the next. Plus, should a shop be left with a particular print from an older collection, it won't look hugely out of place in a more current collection, thus extending its shelf life. —MICHELLE ENGEL BENCSKO

We all live within our own personal palette; it's like having personal style or a specific brand of humor. You are what you are. Everyone sees color in her or his own unique way. Sometimes I will see a palette in a magazine and think, "That's gorgeous—I wanna do that!" I go home, pull color chips, mock it up, and take a step back only to discover that I have managed to make it look exactly like something I have already done. —TULA PINK

I switch it up, but I do tend to go for bright pastels. —BARI J. ACKERMAN

I don't have a go-to palette per se, but I do find myself constantly going back to green/orange combinations. That's sort of my default palette, I guess! Although I vary the greens and oranges a lot. But I do switch it up, too, and I like to challenge myself to use colors that don't come as easily to me—purple, for instance. I love playing around with color—it's my favorite part of being an artist. —JESSICA SWIFT

Do you have a palette of go-to/ brand colors, or do you prefer to switch it up completely between collections? (Or somewhere in between?) Why?

I usually switch my palettes up completely between collections, though I do find that the coral-red color that I use for my logo manages to slip in there often. I like exploring with color, and I find that different palettes suit different collections. However, when I license my art to other fabric manufacturers, I often do not get to choose the final colorways. —JENNIFER MOORE

Probably something in between, though I think I have a very strong color sensibility that comes through in all that I do. I tend to prefer a warmer palette overall, and I like odd combos. —DENYSE SCHMIDT

During the process I stick with my own go-to colors—colors I love and that I am comfortable with. While I am designing the prints, I don't want to be distracted by color, so I keep it familiar. Once I am set, then I play with color, which can really make or break a print. —MO BEDELL

Colorways and Collections

Every type of fabric producer—from hobbyist to major manufacturer—produces single, stand-alone prints, called *one-offs*,
either in one colorway or in several. Creating stand-alone
prints allows experimentation: lots of little ideas that might
otherwise get scrapped can make their way onto fabric.

However, if the fabric is intended for the mass market, it's likely that
the fabric designs will be part of a *collection*, or group of coordinating fabrics. Most fabric buyers shopping with a certain project
in mind seek out coordinates, so why not be the one to design
them and sell them? Users may combine coordinates to sew into
a single item like a quilt or a purse. Or they may use coordinates
to make separate but matching items—a blouse and a skirt; or pillows, drapes, and upholstery to decorate a single room. To please
the widest range of consumer tastes, collections typically bring
together various kinds of motifs that come in a few different *color
stories*—color groups that form collections within the collection.

While collections and color stories are partially market driven,
they also provide the designer with further opportunity to express
him- or herself, to expand a simple vision into a full story. Putting
together collections and color stories is an art with infinite possibilities, but as with other aspects of fabric design, it's not without
some constraints. This section examines just some of the ways
in which designers combine conventions of end use with their
artistic vision to create amazing fabric collections. It also provides
starting points and guidance for creating your own collections.

Color in Collections

Color schemes and palettes, once applied to fabric, are called *col-orways*. You'll hear this term applied both to color variations of the same print and to groups of prints that relate via color to form a distinct group within a larger collection. For clarity's sake, however, I'll use the term *color story* to refer to the latter. Some color stories stand on their own as collections within the collection, yet they also interconnect so that some or all the prints in the wider collection coordinate. Often the color stories in a collection will oppose in some way—warm versus cool, or bright versus pastel, for example.

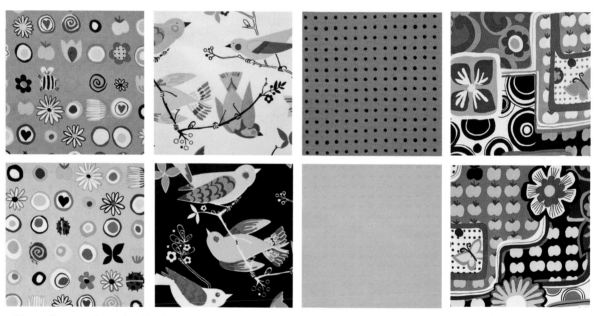

A fabric collection with pastel and bright color stories. The Junebug collection for Alexander Henry Fabrics has a muted, pastel color story (*top row*) and a bright color story (*bottom row*).

Collections and Applications

A useful way to see how design parameters (see Design Parameters, page 10) work to serve a fabric's end use is to look at fabric collections produced for retail fabric's three biggest markets—quilting, home décor, and fashion.

Quilting Cotton Collections

Collections of cotton quilting fabrics can be compact, with only a few prints, or sprawling, with a dozen or more prints in several colorways apiece. They are printed, usually with dyes, onto 45"-wide plain cotton sheeting, and sometimes onto poplin or sateen. (For information about fabrics, see Know Your Surface: Fabric Basics, page 98). Widths up to 110" are sometimes printed for use as quilt backings.

Quilting fabric designs tend to be more whimsical, trendy, colorful, and thematic than fabrics in other types of collections. Many quilters make thematic quilts, for example, for holidays or in honor of a loved one's hobby, so novelty prints are embraced the most here. However, many collections also feature florals and geometrics in the starring roles. Novelty prints often serve as *focus prints* (or *main prints*), so named because they draw the most attention and establish the mood of the collection. Focus prints typically use novelty motifs, higher contrast colors, multiple colors, the juxtaposition of several motifs used throughout the collection, and/or a larger scale.

Scale overall tends toward the smaller end of the spectrum, since they have to look just as good cut up into small pieces as they do coming off the bolt or roll. That being said, many modern quilters enjoy cutting up large-scale prints for special effects.

It's important for quilting collections to offer a balance of small- and large-scale prints, higher contrast and tonal prints, motif types, and flow. These contrasts are all used strategically within the patchwork composition of a quilt or other similar projects. Nondirectional prints are favored, though one- and two-way prints can also work to move the eye around (see Directionality and Orientation, page 10). Since sewists use quilting cottons for a wide variety of applications, today's collections are becoming less formulaic, with less reliance on the focus/support print hierarchy and with a wider range of motifs and styles.

Quilter's Colors

Despite the plethora of color scheme possibilities outlined in Know Your Color (page 58), quilters usually have fewer dividing lines when they describe fabric colorways. Each of the following three colorway types—tonal, analogous, and multicolor—has its own function in the patchwork composition.

Tonal prints use monotonal color schemes, usually two or three shades or tints of the same hue that are close in value. Tonal prints serve as a resting place for the eye, and depending on value contrast and scale of the motifs, can read as solids from a distance.

Analogous prints use analogous color schemes, such as a combination of red, orange, and yellow. These fabrics attract the eye without being overwhelming.

Multicolor prints are higher contrast, energetic, and attention getting. A multicolor print can range from an analogous complementary scheme to a full-on, every-color-of-the-rainbow affair.

Tonal print. From Nature Elements by Patricia Bravo for Art Gallery Fabrics

Analogous color print. From Just Wing It by MoMo for Moda Fabrics

Multicolor print. Twilight Pond from Paradise by Patricia Bravo for Art Gallery Fabrics

Weekends, by Erin McMorris for FreeSpirit Fabrics, is an example of a more eclectic, modern quilting cotton collection. Florals are the star, featured in every print (they're even in the baskets in the bike print). The lack of geometrics and the supporting role of the single novelty print (the bikes) make this collection atypical, but geometric patterns do find their way in as foreground and background fills, and some of the florals do double duty as stripes, dots, and checks. The bicycles even read as dots from a distance. Weekends still has a masterful balance of airy and packed, large and small scale, and graphic and organic lines for which both traditional and modern designers strive.

Overall, Weekends is composed mainly of pure hues and tints of four tertiary colors: yellow-green, yellow-orange, red-orange, and red-violet (see Know Your Color, page 58). There is even a pop of blue-green. Warm browns and tans (basically shades of orange) and gray are used as neutrals. There is a lot of interchangeability between the colorways.

Overall the palette of tertiary colors is harmonious, with light fuschia tying all three colorways together.

Nice balance of large, medium, and small scale motifs.

The more graphic florals play the role of geometrics, as do the simple geometric pattern fills in the floral prints.

A FIELD GUIDE TO FABRIC DESIGN

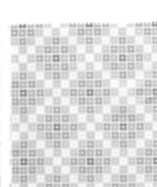

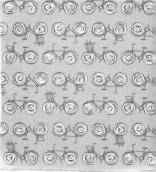

Smaller-scale novelty print takes a back seat to the florals-unusual but clever.

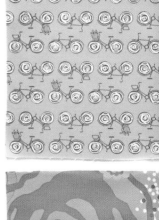

Most designs packed; the spaced designs are layered over a background pattern for added texture and interest in patchwork projects.

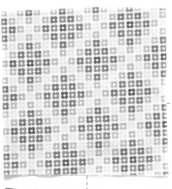

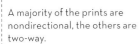

A majority of the prints are nondirectional, the others are two-way.

COLORWAYS AND COLLECTIONS

While the style of Just Wing It, by MoMo for Moda Fabrics, is graphic and modern, it represents a timeless assemblage of print types for a quilting collection. Its focus print brings together just about every motif found throughout the collection, only at a larger scale. It is slightly atypical in that few geometrics are used. The one classic geometric print is the pinstripe, which also serves as a tonal (in fact it is as near to a solid as you can get without being a true solid). The half-drop patterns of trees and four-leaf clovers provide stronger lines in contrast to the more flowing designs, and as such they serve the role usually played by geometrics. Directionality, spacing, and scale are all in perfect balance. Supporting prints have mostly monochromatic or analogous color schemes, some with accents of a complementary color. In a patchwork composition this would serve as a backdrop that makes the multicolor focus and secondary prints really pop.

Chartreuse unites the bright, multicolor palette.

Though butterflies are considered a novelty motif, they are a classic one, which makes Just Wing It a very versatile collection with wide appeal.

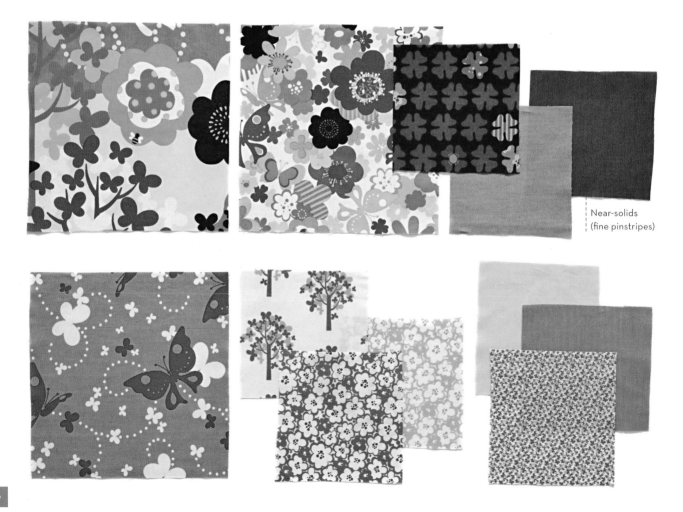

Near-solids
(fine pinstripes)

Multicolor, large-scale focus prints relate to multiple sets of supporting prints.

Continuous print

Scale ranges from tiny to superscale with everything in between.

Balance of packed and spaced prints, directional and non-directional, flowy and set patterns.

Free to Grow, by Nancy Mims for Robert Kaufman Fabrics, is typical of quilting cotton collections in that it has a pleasing balance of small-, medium-, and large-scale prints; of floral and geometric prints; and of regimented stripes and undulating, curvy lines. Tonal prints anchor the multicolor prints. Even the multicolor prints are composed mainly of monotone or analogous color combinations with little pops of contrast, so no attention hogs steal the limelight in a patchwork project. The three color stories are distinctive yet have some interrelationship, so there are plenty of choices to please both warm- and cool-leaning tastes.

This collection is atypical in that it has no novelty prints and no single focus print, and it has more directional prints than usual. This reflects Mims' background as a home décor fabric designer; in fact, some of the Free to Grow prints are adaptations of designs originally created for her organic home décor company, Mod Green Pod. However, in a quilt, the two-way prints would work cut lengthwise or crosswise, and the one-way floral would work right side up and upside down. Most of the prints have similar spacing on solid backgrounds, but that's an aesthetic choice by the designer that doesn't affect functionality. (It's also an atypical collection in that it was the very first 100% organic cotton print collection from a major manufacturer.)

Colorways stand apart with distinct look and feel, yet are interrelated, so buyers can mix and match and avoid "matchy-matchy" syndrome.

Medium-scale, multicolor florals (together with large-scale floral) serve as "focus prints," a role often played by novelty prints.

"SUMMER" colorway is bright and warm, dominated with pink with pops of yellow.

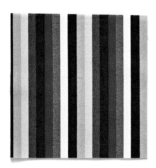

Large scale floral echoed on a smaller scale
and layered over scrollwork geometric print

"GARDEN" colorway
is also bright and
warm overall; green
(which is sometimes
said to be neither
cool nor warm)
acts as a neutral.

Simple stripes can bring
together all colors used
in the colorway.

Stripe is cleverly echoed
in a flowy floral.

Large-scale floral

"SPRING" colorway
is cool and earthy,
infused with hints
of warmth from
the yellow.

Mixture of ornate/fluid and
regimented geometrics

COLORWAYS AND COLLECTIONS

Home Décor Collections

Traditional home décor collections are sold in specialty interior design stores (sometimes to-the-trade only) and in chain fabric stores. A traditional collection includes several different fabrics of varying weights in coordinating colors for specific end uses—such as sheers for curtains; heavy, textured, woven solids and jacquards for upholstery; and multipurpose prints for upholstery and pillows. But recently there has been a trend toward modern home décor collections composed entirely of prints. These collections are usually produced by smaller, independent companies and quilting cotton manufacturers. These fabrics, printed on wide (60"+), heavier-weight cottons, laminates, and other natural fibers, are sometimes too lightweight for upholstery. But by sacrificing this one application, several others are gained, including accessories, quilts, and even apparel.

Generally, scale in home dec fabric designs is larger and showier than that used for quilting or apparel fabrics. Because people usually live with their home décor fabric choices for a long time, motifs and colors tend toward the classic and timeless. (In fact, most home décor fabrics have a longer shelf life than typical quilt and fashion prints.)

Paula Smail creates all the fabrics for Henry Road, her design studio and store based in Los Angeles. The predominance of floral and geometric motifs in her collections is typical for home dec, but Smail's design style is much more expressive and lively than that of traditional home décor patterns. Most of the designs are spaced, rather than closely packed, on boldly colored backgrounds.

The color palette is not strictly coordinated between prints, but Smail mixes and matches colors and prints in a line of accessories and finished home décor items that she also creates. Most prints a nondirectional, though of all applications, home dec is the easiest realm in which to use directional prints. (Drapes and furniture have a fixed top and bottom, so one- and two-way prints are a natural fit

Henry Road fabrics are atypical of home décor collections in several ways. They are of a smaller scale than typical home dec store fare (though the scale is much larger than the average fashion or quilting print). There is no strict line dividing main prints from coordinates. Their colors are much bolder than those of most home dec fabrics. Taken as a collection, they are united more by style than by anything else.

Prints offered in various scales, reflecting versatile end uses

Basecloth is a heavy cotton canvas.

Motifs are medium to large scale; the butterfly is the smallest at about 1 square inch.

FLORALS

"Daisy" (a smaller scale floral) and "Gloria" (a bold, graphic, stylized floral) come in neutrals and a range of colors to suit any decor.

Though "Fish" and "Blossom" are technically novelties, the motifs are classic and organic. Trees and butterflies are almost florals, and the fish is rendered so simply and boldly, it borderlines on a geometric.

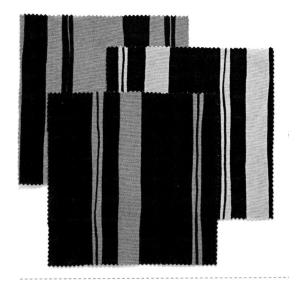

GEOMETRICS

A classic, simple stripe or something as simple as a dot can still reflect the designer's distinctive style.

Fashion Collections

Although fashion fabrics have always been a fixture in retail fabric stores, they have not usually been marketed as brand-name coordinating collections. Recently, however, brand-name, designer fashion fabric collections have begun to emerge on the retail market. These modern collections offer topweights (such as voile, lawn, and knits) and bottomweights (such as twill, corduroy, and velveteen) and a variety of prints, solids, and textures—all of which can be assembled into a complete, coordinated look. Fabrics are usually 45" or 60" wide. Motif and style differences depend on the end use of the fabric—for women's wear, children's wear, or menswear.

Women's wear is the biggest market for fashion fabrics. Florals, small-scale geometrics, and classic novelty motifs such as birds and butterflies are always popular; other novelty motifs are more subject to trends, and their appeal may be limited to niche markets. Keeping the scale small to medium and color palettes subdued ensures the widest appeal. But if you look on the fashion runways, you will see a mind-blowing array of inventive prints that run the gamut of color, scale, motif, and style. Women's fashion offers the opportunity to really go wild.

Children's and teens' wear. Sewing moms (and dads!) are a growing market, so kids' apparel prints are beginning to rival, if not overtake, women's wear prints in popularity. Novelty prints sit better with younger fashions. Classic boys' motifs include sports, transportation, dinosaurs, and outer space. Classic girls' motifs (outside of florals) include ballerinas, dolls, and hearts. However, modern collections are trending toward more gender-neutral themes (such as animals) and edgier, more rebellious motifs (such as tattoos and skulls). Though pastels and pink for girls and blue and green for boys continue to dominate fabric design, there is also a trend toward more gender-neutral schemes based on red, orange, or green and more age-neutral motifs and styles that can grow with the child.

Menswear. The market for home sewing men's clothing isn't huge, and solids, tweeds, pinstripes, stripes, and plaids dominate what market there is. However, that's not to say you can't design versatile prints that are menswear-suitable.

Liberty of London. This is one company that has been producing coordinating, brand-name fashion fabric collections for decades. Their fabrics are known for their quality and distinctive, classic, yet fashion-forward, designs. Liberty produces sprawling collections of new prints on their signature Tana Lawn fabric twice yearly and also rereleases classic prints in new colorways. Collections include different color stories, though with a lot of interrelatedness.

Liberty's Autumn 2010 collection, only a portion of which is pictured here, was inspired by Japan and includes fabrics by internationally renowned guest designers Minä Perhonen and Angie Lewin. It wouldn't be Liberty without florals, and this collection is no exception. Bigger, showier, and more expressive designs join the classic Liberty small-scale, packed florals. The darker colorways of the novelty prints force the viewer to look twice to discern anime characters or a Tokyo cityscape. Despite the weighty, cold-weather palette, a distinct theme of airiness runs through the collection—tossed prints; feathery, delicate lines; and windblown motifs.

There is not really such a thing as "typical" when it comes to fashion in general, but these prints never stray from the small-to-medium scale. Most of the prints are also packed or have patterned backgrounds, adding a textural quality, especially when viewed from afar. This collection includes several one- and two-way prints, which is unusual, but here the artistry definitely takes precedence over the flexibility that tossed prints would offer. Besides, Liberty fabrics are relatively expensive, which gears them toward experienced sewists who know how to handle directional prints.

Unlike typical quilting and home décor fabric collections, and unlike the modern fashion collections of top- and bottomweights (page 102), these prints are related more by style; coordination is not a great concern. Certainly, more than one print can be used in a garment (e.g., a main print with contrasting trim), but no strong hierarchy of focus and supporting prints is found here as it is in other types of collections. The prints are "equal players," reflecting fashion sewists' tendencies to purchase one print per garment.

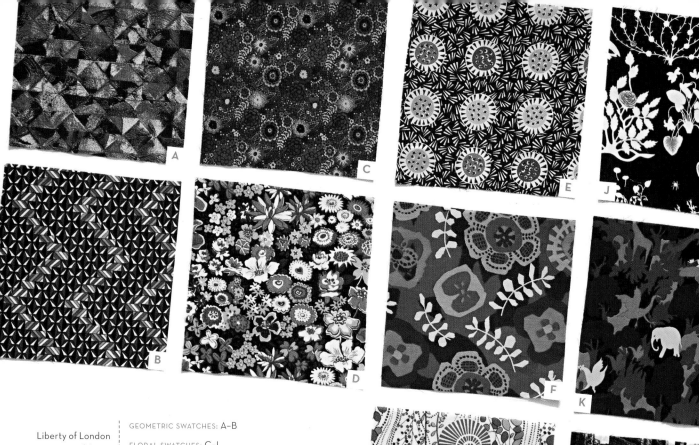

Liberty of London fabrics

GEOMETRIC SWATCHES: A–B

FLORAL SWATCHES: C–I

NOVELTY PRINT SWATCHES: J–N

GEOMETRIC PRINTS: These geometrics would work for men's and women's wear. (A, B)

SMALL-SCALE FLORAL: Liberty is best known for their packed, colorful, small-scale florals, so no seasonal collection would be complete without them. (C, D)

SQUARE REPEAT SET PATTERN: Unusual for fashion prints but the scale, color, and textural background of this print by guest artist Angie Lewin makes this print work. (E)

AIRY, ORGANIC DESIGNS: These airy, organic designs suit the light, drapey Tana Lawn basecloth and the flowy fashions for which they are suited. (F, G, H, I, J, N)

DIRECTIONAL PRINTS: Most are two-way or nondirectional. (G, H, J, K, L)

WHIMSICAL NOVELTY PRINTS: Wilder, more whimsical novelty prints in Liberty's seasonal collections could work for kids' clothing and unique women's wear. (K, L, M)

Designing Your First Collection

As you gain experience with designing individual fabrics, you may feel inspired to move on to designing an entire collection. The collections presented in these pages are meant to serve as guidelines, not formulas. In this new era of fabric design, I expect you to creatively and strategically flout the conventions!

Once you have decided on the market for your proposed collection, the seed for the design of the fabric collection can come from several sources. A theme, a phrase, a feeling, or a concept might come first. Or you might start with a more tangible inspiration, like a song or film, a historical figure, a loved one, a painting, or a keepsake. Some designers seek to evoke design styles of a particular culture or era. Whatever it is, use it to provide a starting point for the motifs and colors. Brainstorm by yourself and with others, jotting down things that are associated with your central inspiration. Gather visual inspiration and references in the form of clippings, photos, and sketches.

You might find yourself with several ideas for prints, but even if you have just one, get started. As you work, new prints have a way of suggesting themselves. Motifs that don't work in one print might branch off into the perfect coordinate.

Use the guidelines for the different types of collections (see Collections and Applications, pages 83–94), always keeping contrast and balance in mind, as you decide where to start. For example, if you have a large-scale floral print finished, you might consider a smaller-scale geometric as a starting point for your next print. For supporting prints, start with the set design types described in Design Parameters (page 10) and try to come up with creative variations that fit into your collection. Envision end uses for your fabrics-to-be, and design toward that product's different components. For example, if your floral was made into a cushion, what fabric would look good as piping? If it was made into a bag, what should the lining look like?

Finally, always keep in mind that successful collections do not result from checking off characteristics from a list. (Do I have a large-scale design and a small-scale design? Check. Do I have a spaced design and a packed design? Check.) Instead, they come from striking a balance so that your prints work together and express your creative vision in a way that's satisfying to *you*.

Creating Color Stories

Most designers start with a single color story, which evolves simultaneously with their designs. Sometimes the starting point for color comes from the theme of the collection, but other times, color decisions are independent of the theme. Perhaps the designer establishes a multicolor focus print first, and then draws a few colors from it to use in supporting prints. Sometimes a new design will call for additional colors that aren't part of the working scheme or palette, so the designer expands the color scheme accordingly.

Once a single color story is complete, it can be transformed into new ones (perhaps using the Illustrator color tools featured on page 72). Sometimes these new color stories harmonize with the original, but they certainly don't have to.

Developing multiple, expansive, and harmonious color schemes that work successfully with your designs—especially if you have to keep spot colors consistent for volume printing methods (see page 145)—is one of the biggest challenges of fabric design. In fact, some fabric companies take the lead on color, even staffing color specialists. In addition to the ability to develop and apply complex color palettes, colorists also understand market trends and the technicalities of the printing process, so they can work with you to make choices that best ensure the success of your collection.

For your first foray into multiple color stories, it may be best to start designing your collection with a restricted palette in mind (say, one to five colors) and limit yourself to two color stories. Try reversing the proportions of each color for the new color story, or use tints, shades, or tones of the original palette. Or, let color theory be your guide. For example, if you have a pink-dominant color story, start with its complement (green) as the dominant color in the new color story. (You might decide to make a complementary triad by adding a yellow-orange–dominant color story, or a square tetrad by adding a blue-violet–dominant story, and so on.)

Where to Take Your Collections

If you are seeking to license your designs with a fabric manufacturer to produce a retail fabric collection, your best bet (at this writing) is to structure your collection for quilting applications. More quilting collections are produced annually than any other type of fabric collection. Quilting companies have started producing fashion and home décor collections, and they have not been market-proven like quilting cottons, so their future is uncertain. To further ensure their success in this experimental phase, these nonquilting collections from quilting manufacturers are usually created by established designers with a built-in following. At this time, there's a chance that approaching a quilting company with, say, a cotton knit collection or large-scale home décor print would help you stand out favorably, but more likely your work would be viewed as being too narrowly focused. For more on licensing your collections to more exclusively fashion- and home décor–focused manufacturers, see Other Licensing Avenues (page 150).

A lot of untested waters remain within the digital printing route (see Digital Printing, page 134). Some digital textile printing services offer the ability to sell designs directly through their websites. (This allows the designer to earn a commission or credits that can be applied toward their own fabric purchases. When your designs sell, you can get cash, or credit to buy fabric from the printer.) Alternatively, the designer can sell them on his or her own. The variety of different base cloths offered by these printers provides a great opportunity for the individual designer to create either narrowly focused or multipurpose collections.

PRINTING

A FIELD GUIDE TO FABRIC DESIGN

Fabric Basics

You understand from the Design and Color section of this book how to create patterns, but before you delve into printing techniques, it's important to understand and appreciate fabric—the surface that inspires and guides the fabric designer's work. This chapter is devoted to the basics of fabric construction, the types of fibers from which fabric is made, and the more fine-grained distinctions among commonly printed fabrics.

Familiarity with the characteristics and qualities of base cloths (the base upon which you print) will help to ensure that you have a successful printing venture. This is true whether you are printing digitally or using DIY techniques, or whether you are licensing your designs (and are in the enviable position of having input on the choice of base cloth). The intended end use, together with the cost and availability, will narrow down your field of fabric candidates significantly. Printing methods also govern your choice: Digital printers tend to work with certain types of fabric; and for DIY methods, some fabrics are more suitable than others. From there, it's mostly about preference in regard to texture and about how your prints work in conjunction with the cloth (which can, for better or worse, only be discovered through experimentation).

A Look at Fabric Construction

Fabrics are constructed in three basic ways:
They can be woven, knit, or nonwoven.

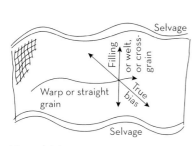

Woven fabric

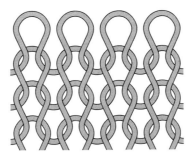

Knit fabric

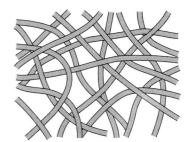

Nonwoven fabric

Woven Fabrics

When you think of fabric, you usually picture a woven fabric, which is constructed on a loom. The loom is first loaded with *warp yarns* (they're called yarns, even though they're usually thinner than sewing thread). These yarns become the lengthwise grain (straight grain) of the fabric. They have to be strong enough to withstand being stretched and pulled back and forth. Then *weft*, or *filling*, yarns are woven over and under the warp yarns. These yarns form the cross grain of the fabric. They are typically not as strong as the warp yarns and have a little stretch to them.

No matter what printing method you're using, you want to make sure the print is *on grain*, not skewed relative to the warp or weft threads. When sewists cut out fabric, especially for garments, they are careful to cut fabrics on grain; otherwise, the garment doesn't hang correctly on the wearer's body. Grain is also important for knit fabrics, even though they don't have a warp and weft.

The *bias* is an imagined line that runs diagonally across the fabric. Fabric cut on the bias (the "true bias" is 45°) is very stretchy. Cutting on the bias can be useful for making trim that goes around corners and curves or for making garments that drape and swirl.

The *selvage* is formed along the edges of the fabric, where the weft yarns turn to travel back across the warp. This area is woven more tightly than the main body of the fabric for stability throughout the manufacturing process. (When sewing, you usually cut off the selvages.) A fabric's identifying information is printed on the selvage. Lately, quilters have had fun using selvage strips in scrappy patchwork projects, and designers have responded by making the selvages just as beautiful as the fabric's main print.

Information printed on the selvage was once purely functional. Now designers are starting to get creative, adding their logos and using motifs from the design as color spots.

Understanding the three basic weaves and their variations is the key to understanding the differences among fabrics. The weave determines surface texture and sheen and contributes to strength, drape, and other factors.

Plain weave is the most basic type. Each weft yarn travels over and then under adjacent warp yarns. This fabric tears and wrinkles easily, but it provides an excellent base for printing.

Twill weave refers to any of a number of variations in which each weft yarn travels over two or more warp yarns and then passes under the warp yarns. The pattern is staggered for each weft yarn, creating distinct diagonal lines on the finished fabric. Herringbone and houndstooth are variations of the basic twill weave. Twills are very strong and difficult to rip.

Satin weave is a type in which either the warp or weft yarns are the "face," floating over four or more of the opposite yarns before passing under one, and then floating over four or more and then under one again. Unlike twills, the intersections do not form a diagonal pattern. The satin weave yields a very lustrous surface and is also highly tear-resistant.

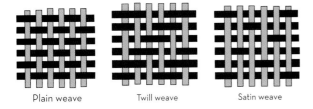

Plain weave   Twill weave   Satin weave

Pile fabrics are made by looping an extra set of yarn through a woven or knit base. The loops are then cut (as they are with velvet, velveteen, and corduroy) or can remain uncut (as in terry cloth).

Knits

Knits are constructed from one continuous piece of yarn that is interlooped. There are several types of knit fabrics, depending on how they are stitched. Columns of stitches are called wales, and rows are called courses. Typically, knit fabrics are more stretchy and drapey than wovens. Though knits are a common base cloth for traditional mass production and digital printing, and printing on knit T-shirts is a big industry, knit yardage is not a great candidate for DIY printing methods because of its stretchiness. With knits, like wovens, you want to make sure that your directional prints are on grain with the wales and courses.

Nonwovens

Nonwovens are formed from loose fibers that are naturally matted (such as wool felt) or chemically adhered together (such as synthetic felt). You don't often see mass-produced printed felt, and I've not yet seen it as a base cloth for digital printing, but there's no reason not to use it with hand-printing methods. Since this fabric has no grain and does not ravel or roll up when cut, you don't have to worry about printing on grain.

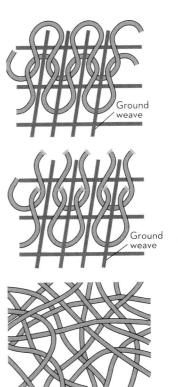

Ground weave

Ground weave

Loop pile, cut pile, and nonwoven structures

Fiber Types

Fabrics are made of plant, animal, or synthetic fibers.

Cotton is the most popular and widespread of all fibers. It's versatile, strong, cool, absorbent, and easy to care for and work with. It's also available in a wide variety of weaves and textures.

Other plant-based fibers include linen, which is made from the flax plant; hemp, made from a similar plant whose fibers are rougher than linen unless further processed; and rayon, which sits on the fence between a natural and a synthetic fiber. Its fibers are derived from the cellulose of wood or plants (including bamboo) and then processed. Rayon is also known as viscose and Modal (a version trademarked by Lenzing AG). These plant-based fabrics are more expensive than cotton but less expensive than animal fibers.

Animal fibers include silk, which is a filament (a single, fine thread) harvested from unreeled cocoons of the silkworm. Silk is mostly associated with women's wear and accessories like scarves and ties, but heavier, firmer silks can also be made into bags, home décor items, and quilts.

Wool and other animal hair fibers like camel hair and cashmere are rarely printed. Theoretically, you could print onto wool using fiber-reactive or acid dyes (thickened if screen-printing) or pigments, though the latter may not survive abrasion or washing.

Synthetics, whether 100% synthetic or synthetic-blend fabrics including polyester, acrylic, nylon, and spandex, are made by using several types of manufactured fibers. Retail synthetic fabrics usually do not have their own nomenclature but are marketed as inexpensive versions of familiar natural fabrics; for example, charmeuse, sateen, or broadcloth. However, some special synthetic fabrics are featured later in this chapter.

Though synthetic fabrics are the least expensive on the retail market, as a digital printing base cloth they are typically more expensive than cotton.

Fabric Weight

End use and fabric weight go hand in hand. The most delicate projects call for lightweight fabrics; projects that will undergo lots of use, cleaning, and wear need tough, heavy fabrics. Between those ends of the spectrum are a myriad of project types, each with its own range of suitable weights. Following is a guide to the terminology used in describing fabric weight.

With the exception of silk, which has its own system, fabric weight is usually expressed as ounces per square yard (or grams per square meter). *Note: Be aware that sometimes the weight is measured per linear yard or meter, which can be misleading.*

Sometimes a fabric supplier may only describe the weight in subjective terms—as light- or handkerchief weight (less than 4 oz.), medium weight (approximately 4–6 oz.), or heavyweight (more than 6 oz.). Sometimes the supplier might not know the weight at all. For apparel fabrics, top-weight, bottomweight, and coating weight are also used to subjectively describe fabrics.

In general, the most lightweight fabrics (top-weights) are typically used for apparel (blouses, scarves, and sometimes skirts). Medium- to heavyweights (also known as bottomweights) are also used for pants and skirts. Medium weights are best for quilts, accessories, and crafts. Heavyweights are used in home décor, especially for upholstery, since upholstered furniture must stand up to the greatest wear.

Silk is measured in *momme,* which is abbreviated as *mm*—and I won't blame you if you continue to confuse the abbreviation with "millimeter" even after learning this fact. Eight momme equals 1 ounce, so divide the momme weight by 8 to convert it to the more familiar ounces per square yard. Lightweight silk is approximately 20 mm and below; medium weight is 20–28 mm, and heavyweight is greater than 28 mm.

Yarn Weight and Quality

For woven fabrics, weight is determined by the yarn weight and density of the weave. If you source base fabrics wholesale, you may encounter terms related to these characteristics, as well as terms related to yarn quality. You are probably familiar with *thread count* from buying bedsheets. Although sheet thread counts as advertised are sometimes purposely misleading, it is true that higher counts equal higher quality. Count is expressed as the number of warp yarns and weft yarns per square inch; for instance, 68 × 68 is a standard count for high-quality quilting cottons.

Yarn size (for spun fibers like cotton and wool) or *denier* (for filament fibers like silk and synthetics) describes the thickness of the yarn; higher numbers indicate finer yarns.

Understanding PFD Fabrics

The ideal fabrics to use for hand-printing methods are labeled *prepared for dye* (PFD) or *prepared for printing* (PFP).

When weaving all kinds of fabric, a natural or synthetic chemical called *sizing* is applied to the warp yarns to help them withstand the rigors of the loom. Before these fabrics can be printed, the sizing has to be removed for dyes to properly react to the fibers or for pigment inks to best adhere. This removal process yields PFD fabrics.

Technically, PFP fabric is even cleaner and therefore yields higher quality prints, but it's difficult to find retail. PFD fabric should do just fine for hobby and cottage industry printing. PFD and PFP fabrics are a natural beige or white.

Unlike *dyes*, which chemically react with fibers and become part of their structure, *pigments* are colored particles that adhere on the surface to fibers through binding agents. So while PFD/PFP fabrics provide the ideal base for printing, you're in no way limited to them if printing with pigments. Pigment inks can adhere to almost any predyed and preprinted fabrics of any fiber type, assuming there is no coating such as lamination. To have the best chance at a colorfast print, though, prewash all fabrics in hot water and mild laundry soap (do not use detergents with optical brighteners, scents, or other such additives).

If you're hand printing (see Step-by-Step Hand Printing, page 110), a good guideline to follow is that if it's tricky to sew, it's also tricky to print. Avoid loose weaves, sheers, and very drapey or shifty fabrics until you really know what you're doing.

Do not confuse *greige* fabrics with PFD/PFP. Greige fabrics are those in their predyed or preprinted state, but greige goods come straight off the loom and have not had the sizing or impurities removed—so they have low dye affinity, and pigments inks may not adhere properly. However, *bleached* fabrics and *mercerized* fabrics have improved dye affinity and are fine for printing too. Mercerization is a process of applying a chemical finish applied to cotton fabric that increases its strength and shine.

Voile

Lawn

Gauze

Broadcloth

Quilting cotton

Muslin

Flannel

Commonly Printed Fabrics

Cotton

Note: Fabrics are shown roughly in order of average weight.

Voile
PFD D
Sheer plain-weave fabric woven from tightly twisted, fine yarns. Most suitable for apparel.

Lawn
PFD D
Semisheer to opaque, high-count plain-weave fabric usually made with combed yarns. Ideal for apparel; also used for quilts and accessories.

Gauze
PFD
Very loosely woven, sheer plain-weave fabric. Double gauze—two layers attached with tiny, intermittent stitches—is a popular base cloth among Japanese manufacturers. This light, drapey, and soft yet opaque fabric is suitable for apparel, crafts, and quilting.

Broadcloth
PFD D
Tightly woven plain-weave shirting fabric with tiny crosswise ribs.

Quilting cotton
PFD D
Plain-weave, medium-weight fabric. Available in a huge variety of prints, solids, and yarn-dyes (the yarns are dyed before they are woven on the loom). Look for *cotton sheeting*—which is another term for plain-weave cotton, not to be confused with cotton bedsheets—for hand and digital printing.

Muslin
PFD
Unbleached, undyed, and unprinted plain-weave fabric. Available in a variety of qualities, weights, and widths. Often used for more utilitarian purposes like garment mock-ups and foundations for patchwork.

Flannel
PFD
Plain-weave cotton (sometimes twill) with soft, lofty texture achieved by a brushing process. Used for shirting and bedding.

Some of the fabrics included here are usually only printed with mass production methods, but most of them are available as base cloths for digital printing or can be purchased for hand printing.

LEGEND

D = available for printing from digital printing bureaus

 = recommended for hand-printing methods

PFD = widely available PFD*

 = commonly printed via volume-production methods

* Fabrics listed as PFD but lacking a are better suited for free-form design techniques, such as painting or dyeing, or for printing by experienced printers.

Jersey knit

Sweatshirt fleece

Interlock knit

Poplin

Corduroy

Sateen/satin

Velveteen

Twill

Canvas and duck

Jersey knit

PFD 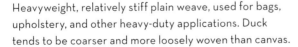 Hand-knitting equivalent is knit stockinette stitch (knit stitches on the front, purls on the back—so there is a right and a wrong side). Has a crosswise stretch. Used for apparel.

Interlock knit

PFD D Closest hand-knitting equivalent is ribbed stitch; does not have a right or wrong side (unless printed). Usually thicker and better quality than jersey. Has a crosswise stretch. Used for apparel.

Poplin

PFD D Tight, strong rib weave using thicker or multiple warp yarns. Close to broadcloth but a bit heavier. Used for all kinds of apparel; a good all-purpose fabric.

Sateen/satin

PFD D Fine, high-count fabric; its distinctive shine comes from the satin weave. Sateen has weft floats, and satin has warp floats. Used for apparel, home décor, and crafts.

Corduroy

Plain pile weave constructed with an extra set of weft yarns, which are cut and brushed into distinctive wales. Printed corduroys are often fine wale. Weight varies; applications range from shirting to upholstery.

Velveteen

PFD The cotton version of velvet is another type of pile weave (though closer cut and not as lush as velvet). Multipurpose—can be used for apparel, crafts, and home décor.

Twill

PFD D Various kinds of fabric woven with a twill weave. Strong, durable, does not rip. Uses range from pants and skirts to upholstery, depending on weight. Denim, gabardine, and chino are twills.

Canvas and duck

PFD D Heavyweight, relatively stiff plain weave, used for bags, upholstery, and other heavy-duty applications. Duck tends to be coarser and more loosely woven than canvas.

Sweatshirt fleece

PFD This medium-weight fabric has a jersey knit face and a napped back. The napped side lends sturdiness, which makes this fabric easier to hand print than other knits.

Rayon challis

Crinkle rayon

Linen

Wool felt

Hemp

Silk chiffon/georgette

Nylon-Lycra

Polyester fleece

China silk/habotai

Silk crepe

Silk
charmeuse/satin

Dupioni silk

Other plant-based fibers

Linen
PFD ✋ D ▟

Strong, absorbent, cool, lint-free fabric; has no stretch. Takes dye and printing easily; natural color also has many fans. Weight ranges from light/handkerchief up to upholstery, with an attendant range of uses.

Hemp
PFD ✋

Commonly blended with other fibers; a good eco-friendly choice.

Rayon challis
PFD D ▟

A fine, plain-woven, silky, light- to medium-weight fabric. Used for apparel.

Crinkle rayon
PFD D ▟

Silky, gauzy fabric with a characteristic wrinkly texture. Used for apparel.

Animal fibers

Silk chiffon/ georgette
PFD D ▟

Plain-weave, very lightweight, sheer fabrics woven with crepe (tightly twisted) yarns for a rough-yet-pleasant texture. Georgette is slightly heavier than chiffon. Difficult to sew; used for women's wear and scarves.

China silk/ habotai
PFD D ▟

Lightweight, smooth fabric, with a lustrous plain weave.

Silk crepe
PFD D ▟

Heavy, opaque plain weave using crepe yarns, which yield a distinct rough-yet-soft texture.

Silk charmeuse/ satin
PFD D ▟

Opaque, shiny; the ultimate drapey fabric, distinguished by a satin weave.

Dupioni silk
PFD ✋ ▟

Medium- to heavyweight, firm, plain-weave fabric made with thick, irregular, "slubby" weft yarns. Lighter weights can be used for apparel; heavier weights are often used in home décor and crafts.

Wool felt
PFD ✋

A nonwoven, sturdy fabric that is great for stuffed toys and other crafts and for home décor items such as coasters and placemats. Has no grain and does not ravel. Available in several thicknesses; also available in less expensive wool/rayon blends.

Synthetics

Polyester fleece
PFD ✋ D ▟

Thickly napped yet lightweight knitted or woven polyester fabric. Used for blankets, hats, jackets, cloth diapers. Beware of lower-quality fleece, which is prone to pilling.

Nylon-Lycra
D ▟

Four-way stretch fabric used for athletic wear and most women's swimwear. Lycra is a trademarked version of spandex filament yarn.

ECO-CONSCIOUS CHOICES

Unfortunately, cotton is environmentally unfriendly when conventionally farmed—it requires heavy fertilizer and pesticide use. Furthermore, the cotton industry has always been controversial from an economic and labor standpoint. However, the demand for organic and fair-trade cotton is on the rise, and the industry worldwide is showing signs of improvement. Linen, which is made from the multipurpose flax plant, is relatively gentle on the environment compared with cotton, as is hemp. Also, the processing that wood cellulose fibers undergo to become rayon fabric may be polluting to the environment.

2011 by *True Up*

A FIELD GUIDE TO FABRIC DESIGN

Step-by-Step Hand Printing

For your first prints on fabric, DIY methods are fun, Luddite-friendly, and provide the most instant gratification. Though there are many ways to decorate the surface of cloth, the design styles that speak to me most are created with the regular, repeatable, durable, graphic printing methods: block printing and screen printing. Even with a small temporary "studio" set up at your kitchen table, you can produce several yards at a time with these methods.

Block printing is by far the cheapest and easiest entry point into fabric printing. Using a block of linoleum or rubber, you carve away the nonprinting areas of your design. Then you roll ink onto the block and press the inked design onto your fabric.

Screen printing is a form of stenciling using a fine-mesh fabric stretched onto a frame. You can adhere low-tech stencils made of paper to screens, but the gold standard for durability and detail is the *photo emulsion stencil*. These are "burned" onto the screen using techniques described in the Screen Printing tutorial (page 119). With this method, ink is pressed through the open areas of the design onto the fabric.

Both block- and screen-printing methods have their own learning curves. It takes experience to achieve clean, consistent impressions, so expect some initial failures and just have fun. The tutorials in this chapter are for printing repeats, but to better ensure a successful print run, beginners may wish to scale back and print free form using blocks or screens containing single motifs, perhaps on smaller pieces of cloth rather than on running yardage.

OTHER METHODS TO TRY

Though this chapter focuses on block and screen printing, I encourage you to explore less regimented methods—such as paper stencils, resist dyeing, direct painting, and needlework—on their own and in combination with other techniques. If you want to use more colors, which tends to equal more headaches with block and screen printing, try coloring your prints freestyle with fabric paints or adding a textural layer with embroidery. Lately, interest has surged in altering preprinted fabric with bleaching, overdyeing, and appliqué; why not print over it too? You can use fabric in an infinite variety of ways to express your point of view just fine.

BLOCK PRINTING

Almost anything can be used for stamping a design onto a surface. On the lower end of durability are cut vegetables, leaves, and foam; and on the higher end are blocks of wood, rubber, and linoleum. In this book, we'll concentrate on rubber and linoleum (lino) blocks, which are both readily available in most art and graphics supply stores. Linoleum comes precut in rectangles ranging from a couple of square inches to a couple of square feet, both mounted onto wood and unmounted, and is also available in rolls. Rubber blocks come in sizes up to about one square foot.

Rubber blocks are seriously fun to work with. Cutting is smooth and easy. Though I prefer to cut designs using a linoleum block cutter and blades, many people use a simple craft knife or scalpel. Since the block is flexible, it could break into pieces if folded or cut too deeply. Also, the surface is more prone to nicks than linoleum.

Mount the carved blocks on thick Plexiglas using E6000 adhesive. Buy Plexiglas sheets from a home improvement store, ideally one that will cut it to size for you for free. Manufacturers recommend using only water-based inks for rubber blocks, but I have used oil-based inks without a problem.

Lino blocks are more difficult to cut, though some types are softer than others. Skilled carvers can get much more detailed and delicate cuts with lino than with rubber, and the relative durability may make the added work worthwhile. The material must be presanded and secured to a table by a clamp or bench hook for cutting. (A bench hook is a sturdy metal plate with metal lips on two sides to wrap around the table and to use as a stop when carving the lino block. Speedball's bench hook can double as a plate for rolling ink.) Warming the lino in the sun or with a household iron makes for smoother cutting; rewarm it periodically as you

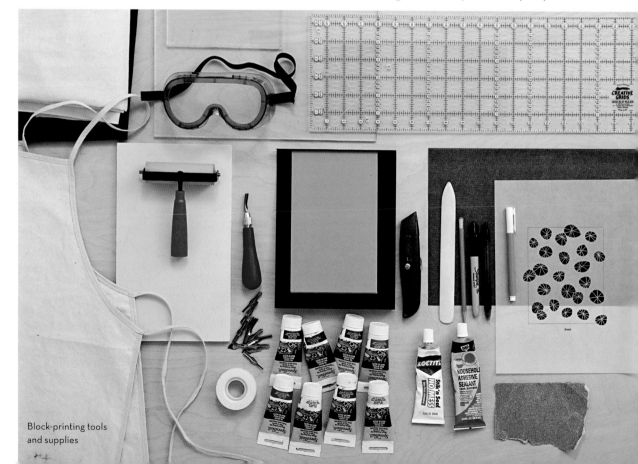

Block-printing tools
and supplies

cut. Linoleum may be purchased unmounted or premounted to wood blocks. Unmounted lino has an advantage for fabric printing because you can cut out the motifs individually and then place and adhere them to transparent Plexiglas that has been marked on its underside with the repeat boundaries.

Lino is thinner than rubber blocks, so the gouge marks left when you carve away the nonprinting areas tend to show up in the print (especially when you're printing on a padded surface, where the block sinks into the base cloth). If you don't like this look, use cut-out pieces mounted on Plexiglas, or choose rubber, which can be cut more deeply.

If this is your first time working with lino cutting, practice on a small piece to get the hang of how the various gouges and line cutters work (hereafter called blades). Practice cutting along curved and intersecting lines and cutting out small areas. Keep your tools sharp, always cut away from your body, and use safety goggles.

This tutorial shows how to print a design with motifs that overlap the repeat boundaries. Printing is done on a padded surface that you can prepare yourself, as described in Creating a Work Surface (page 131).

Choosing Ink

Block-printing inks have a high viscosity, so they stick to the surface of the block without dripping into the nonprinting areas. Oil-based block-printing inks are the best for printing on fabric. Water-based block-printing inks are not wash-fast. However, once printed, oil-based inks must be air-cured for weeks before washing. It is possible to use screen-printing inks, but it takes experimentation with different brands and thickening agents to achieve the necessary viscosity.

Oil-based inks

If working with oil-based inks, make sure you have good ventilation in the room. As an alternative to turpentine or mineral spirits, clean equipment with vegetable oil followed by a nontoxic degreaser.

If the color you want is not available premixed, purchase primary colors and mix them together by hand, using a color wheel (see Using Color Theory, page 62).

MATERIALS

This list includes what you need for both rubber and lino block printing.

- Rubber or linoleum block large enough to contain one full repeat of your design
- Block of wood or Plexiglas on which to mount carved block (*optional*)
- Sharp utility knife if motifs will be cut from the rubber or lino and adhered to wood or Plexiglas
- Bone folder or old butter knife for transferring pencil drawing
- Cellophane tape
- Vellum
- Soft pencil
- Marker
- Linoleum cutter handle and blades
- Brayer
- Small piece of glass, Plexiglas, or metal sheet for rolling ink
- Fabric for printing
- Fabric pen with disappearing or water-soluble ink, available in quilting stores
- Transparent quilting ruler, also available in quilting stores
- Inks (see Choosing Ink, at left)
- Vegetable oil and degreasing cleaner for nontoxic cleanup, if using oil-based ink

FOR LINO ONLY

- Sandpaper
- C-clamps or bench hook
- Graphite transfer paper (*optional*)

Instructions

Preparing the Block

1. Draw a full single repeat of your design or print it from the computer onto a sheet of vellum, including the rectangle indicating the repeat boundaries. This rectangle will serve as a guide to register the design on the block and to transfer the repeat boundary marks to the sides of the block. The transparency of the vellum allows you to place the design over the block, wrong side up, and still see the design for the transfer process in the next step.

2. If using lino, sand the surface of the block; this helps it to hold the ink. Transfer the design to the block by placing a sheet of graphite transfer paper on the block, placing the design over the graphite paper, then tracing over the design with a pencil. I've found that the graphite transfer paper does not work with the softer surface of rubber blocks, though, so you must color in the printing areas with a soft pencil. You can also draw directly on the block, but keep in mind that the image will be reversed in printing. (Figure A)

3. Register the vellum, design side down, to the block. Use the transparent ruler to ensure that the sides of the repeat boundary rectangle are parallel to the edges of the block. Tape the paper to the block. (Figure B)

4. For rubber blocks, transfer the design by rubbing the back of the vellum with the bone folder or the tip of a butter knife. If using graphite paper and lino, trace the design. Lift the paper from the bottom edge to check that the design is transferring thoroughly. Do not yet remove the paper. (Figures C and D)

A   Fill in printing areas to transfer to block.

B   Register design to the block and transfer repeat boundaries.

C

D   Transfer the design.

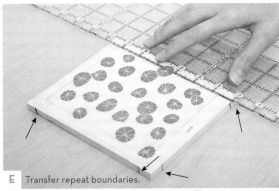

E — Transfer repeat boundaries.

F — Inking over the block

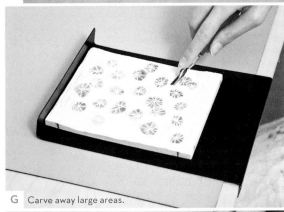

G — Carve away large areas.

H — Detailed carving

5. If the repeat boundaries are smaller than the block, place a ruler against each of the 4 sides of the rectangle, indicating the repeat boundary lines. Make marks on the sides of the block to indicate where these boundary lines will lie. You should end up with 2 marks on each edge of the block. Otherwise, the repeat boundaries are the block corners. (Figure E)

6. When you are finished, remove the design. If there are light or incompletely transferred areas, darken the motifs' outlines on the block with a pen or pencil. (Figure F)

7. If you are using lino, secure it to a tabletop with a clamp or bench hook before carving (no need to do this for rubber). Use the linoleum block carver with the cutting blade of choice. Carve away the nonprinting/background areas of the design with gouges, and then tackle the more detailed areas, curves, and edges with finer line-cutting blades. (Figures G and H)

8. If desired, mount the carved block to Plexiglas (if rubber) or wood (if lino). Whether or not you are mounting the block, label the nonprinting side to indicate which edge is the top. (Figure I)

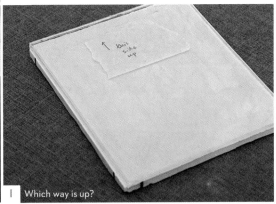

I — Which way is up?

Printing the Fabric

In this process, you will be printing repeats in rows across the width of your fabric.

TIP

Make test prints on scrap fabric first! Areas for troubleshooting may include an uneven printing surface, the design itself, the fabric texture, or the amount or consistency of pressure you apply to the block.

The fabric marker you use to mark the repeat boundaries is crucial—if it is a disappearing ink marker, make sure the marks stay visible through the print run. If you are using a water-soluble marker, test it first to make sure it washes out of your fabric adequately. Also, make marks on dried ink applied to your base cloth to ensure those marks will wash out too.

----

1. Cut or rip the fabric crosswise to ensure a straight and square edge. Iron the fabric and place it on the printing surface. Print crosswise, across the fabric, rather than lengthwise with the selvages. (Figure A)

2. Spread the ink onto the glass, Plexiglas, or other flat surface with the brayer. This helps you to get an even layer of ink for rolling and printing. The brayer should be coated with a thin, even layer. (Figure B)

3. With the brayer, roll the ink onto the block in several crosswise coats. (Figure C)

A   Preparing for printing repeats

B   Coat the brayer.

C   Roll the ink onto the block.

D Print first repeat.

E Transfer marks on fabric corresponding to upper left and lower right marks on block.

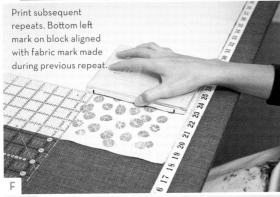

Print subsequent repeats. Bottom left mark on block aligned with fabric mark made during previous repeat.

F

4. Place the block on the lower left corner of the fabric and apply strong, even pressure with your palms. More pressure is needed for linoleum blocks than for rubber blocks. Before lifting the block, place marks on the fabric corresponding to the top left and bottom right marks (on the sides of the block) using the disappearing or water-soluble fabric marker. (Figures D and E)

TIP

If your repeat size equals the block size, your job is a bit simpler. You only need to make marks on the fabric at the corners of the block for a square repeat. This would eliminate the need for a ruler to align the block each time you print.

5. Lift the block, starting on one edge and holding the fabric down. Reapply ink to the block for the next impression. Align the bottom left repeat mark on the printing block with the previous bottom right-hand mark on the fabric. Repeat this process across the width of the fabric. Use the transparent ruler as a guide for vertical alignment—lay the top of the ruler against the top repeat boundary marks on the fabric as shown. If ink gets on the ruler, wipe it off before printing the next repeat. (Figures F, G, and H)

Transfer marks again after printing but before lifting block.

G

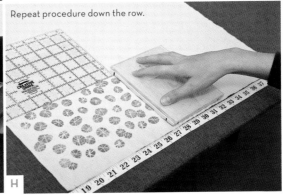

Repeat procedure down the row.

H

6. To print the second row, you align the lower repeat mark on the left edge of the printing block with the vertical repeat mark on the fabric, as shown. Use the ruler to align the marks on the bottom of the block with the corresponding marks from the previous row. Repeat this process for subsequent rows. If your block will print off the fabric in the final row, place scrap paper underneath the fabric so that the block will print on it. (Figures I, J, and K)

7. When finished printing, clean all equipment with vegetable oil and degreaser (for oil-based inks) or water (if using thickened, water-based screen-printing inks.

I Print subsequent rows.

J Making marks after the first print in the second row

K Making the second print in the second row

L Finished fabric

SCREEN PRINTING

Some ways of printing on fabric are far easier, but none are as satisfying as the time-tested technique of screen printing by hand. It's a process full of trial and error (even for experts), but when you finally get it right, the hand-rendered quality of the print and the texture of the ink are wonderful.

The screen-printing process described here uses the photo emulsion method to create a stencil on the screen. Liquid emulsion is applied to a screen, which is a fine polyester mesh stretched onto a frame. A design positive is placed against the dried emulsion and exposed to ultraviolet (UV) light. Emulsion exposed to UV light hardens, but washes out in areas blocked by the opaque areas of the design positive. This creates a stencil for printing. To print, ink is forced through the open areas of the screen with a squeegee.

Very fine detail can be achieved with the photo emulsion method. As with block printing, screen printing can be done using lower-tech ways (for example, a cardstock stencil taped to the screen), but durability is the key here, especially when it comes to printing repeats. For a durable alternative to liquid emulsion that does not require UV light exposure, seek out hand-cut stencil films. You can't achieve as great a level of detail with this type of stencil, but it is faster and simpler than the photo emulsion method.

This tutorial will show you how to print a basic repeat onto a half-width of 45″-wide fabric (which could be cut into and sold as fat quarters). This is a manageable setup for a makeshift home printing studio. Printing onto fabric requires a special padded surface. I've included instructions for building such a surface in Creating a Work Surface (page 131).

Screen-printing supplies and materials

FOR SCREEN PREP

- Screen (Prepare 1 for a test screen; then either reclaim it or prepare a second screen for your final printing.)
- Screen degreaser
- Positive printout of the design
- C-clamp (optional)
- Scoop coater (a couple of inches narrower than your screen's internal height or width)
- Plastic or rubber spatulas
- Metal T-square
- Pencil
- Cellophane tape
- Rags or paper towels
- Photo emulsion made for water-based inks, premixed according to manufacturer's instructions
- Light source (sun can be used)
- Safelight
- Timer

- Glass, cut either slightly smaller than the internal dimensions of the screen or slightly larger than the external dimensions of the screen, depending on exposure setup (see exposure setup option diagrams, page 123)
- Upholstery foam cut to either the internal dimensions of the screen or larger than the external dimensions of the screen, depending on exposure setup (see exposure setup option diagrams, page 123)
- Dark area for drying (cabinet, closet, or cardboard box)
- Pressure washer or a hose with a sprayer nozzle
- Tub for washout
- Blockout pen or small paintbrush
- Emulsion remover
- Gloves
- Scrub brush
- Ventilation mask
- Safety goggles

FOR PRINTING

- T-pins
- Screen tape
- Squeegee (width must be between design width and screen width)
- Water-based inks (see All About Inks, page 130)
- Plastic containers with lids
- Retarder
- Roll of paper or test fabric
- PFD fabric
- Apron to protect clothes
- Printing surface (see Creating a Work Surface, page 131)

Choosing a Screen

Since we're all fabric geeks here, you might appreciate knowing that screen-printing mesh is a plain-weave fabric woven from polyester monofilament thread. The screen mesh count refers to the number of threads crossing per square inch. The higher the number, the finer the mesh, and the finer detail you can achieve. The mesh count you need depends both on the ink you're using and the surface onto which you're printing. For water-based pigment inks and smooth, medium- to heavyweight fabrics, start in the low-to-mid 100s. Go coarser (below 100) if using novelty inks or when printing on textured fabric. Go higher (high 100s to 200s) if printing on very lightweight fabrics. Choose a mesh count between 110 and 155 for smooth, tightly woven fabrics, lower for textured fabrics and higher for lightweight or sheer fabrics. Mesh comes in white and yellow colors; yellow is better for fine detail at higher mesh counts. Aluminum frames are superior to wood, especially for printing with water-based inks.

Preparing the Design Positive

For this tutorial, I am printing along the width of 22½" fabric (45" width of fabric cut in half lengthwise). I used a screen with external dimensions of 30" × 40" for a 16" × 22" repeat, which measured 19½" × 22" after zigzagging the joins (see at right). Your screen size will depend on your design and fabric width, and you can calculate the sizes you need by referring to the chart (page 131).

For your first outing, a one-color, spaced design with bold lines or motifs is ideal. It can get confusing to talk about lengths and widths and edges, so refer to the diagram to get your bearings. Since I am printing across the full width of my fabric (22"), my design only repeats at the top and bottom edges; it wasn't necessary to repeat along the sides.

Include selvage information on the right edge of your design if desired. Also include ¼" registration marks—a cross within a circle—in the selvage at the top and bottom edges of the repeat. You can use blockout fluid to cover them later so they don't print. The print must be as opaque as possible on transparent film,

Rendering Repeats for Hand Printing

Both block-printing and screen-printing techniques require you to create a positive of your design. If your repeat is small and your block or screen is large, you may wish to include several repeats on the positive to make printing more efficient. Do not cut motifs off at the repeat boundaries—that will make registration (aligning the subsequent print impressions) a nightmare. Whenever possible, zigzag the seams as shown to minimize the impact of registration errors.

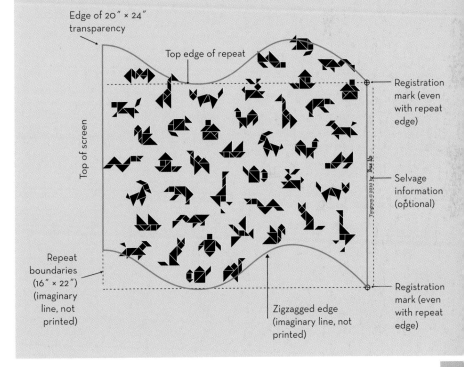

vellum, or matte Mylar (I used the latter in this tutorial). Inquire with local screen-print shops, blueprint services, or architectural printers to print large positives on these substrates.

Preparing the Screen

Degrease the screen by spraying the degreaser onto the dry screen and brushing with a scrub brush. Follow the screen degreaser manufacturer's recommendations on safe handling and disposal. Rinse, and then let the screen dry thoroughly.

COAT THE SCREEN

Coat the screen with photo emulsion in a room with ambient artificial light only (a darkroom with safelight is ideal, but not required).

1. Lean the degreased, dry screen against a door frame and place a C-clamp above the frame, or have a partner hold it in place.

2. Fill the scoop coater half to three-quarters full of emulsion. Hold the scoop coater near the bottom of the screen and tip it toward the screen. Starting on either side of the screen, pull a layer of emulsion up to near the top edge of the screen. At the top, tip the scoop coater back, and shake it side to side to get a smooth finish to the pull. You want all the emulsion to fall back in the trough of the coater and not drip over the edge, because that will make a mess as you add more coats. Even out any blobs with a squeegee, scraping excess back into the emulsion container with each pass. Repeat for another coat and also put 2 coats on the other side of the screen.

3. In a completely dark room, closet, cabinet, or box, lay the screen to dry flat, squeegee/well side up, propped on blocks, so that the photo emulsion doesn't touch anything while it dries. The emulsion is dry when it is no longer tacky to the touch.

REGISTER THE POSITIVE TO THE SCREEN

Complete this step in a darkroom with a safelight, and don't rush, as even slight misalignments can ruin your printing. A closet or a bedroom with blackout shades will also work.

Place your positive on the side of the screen that will be facing the light source (see photo below). It must be right-reading from the squeegee side. With the metal T-square, align the positive's registration marks so that they are perfectly parallel to the outside bottom edge of the frame and tape the positive down securely with transparent cellophane tape (check alignment again after taping to make sure no shifting occurred). Exact horizontal or vertical centering onto the screen is not critical—only that the registration marks are correctly aligned.

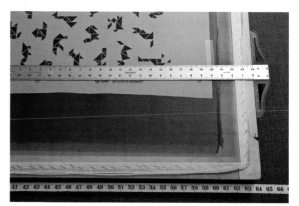

Register positive to screen.

EXPOSE A TEST SCREEN

Create one of the setups shown (below) and expose a test screen. Be *extremely careful* handling glass sheets. For screens larger than a couple of feet in width or length, a professional exposure unit is recommended.

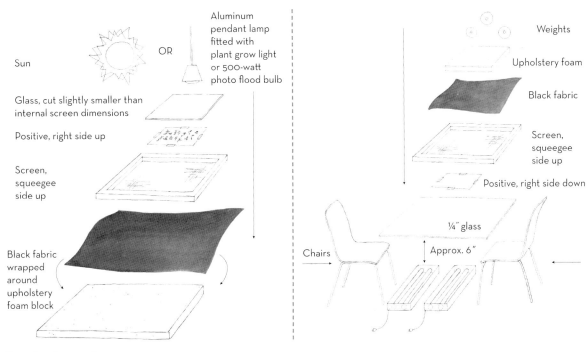

Sun

OR

Aluminum pendant lamp fitted with plant grow light or 500-watt photo flood bulb

Glass, cut slightly smaller than internal screen dimensions

Positive, right side up

Screen, squeegee side up

Black fabric wrapped around upholstery foam block

Weights

Upholstery foam

Black fabric

Screen, squeegee side up

Positive, right side down

¼˝ glass

Chairs

Approx. 6˝

Two setups for exposing screens

Too many variables, including emulsion brand and thickness, screen size, design positive type, and light source, prevent giving even a ballpark estimate of exposure time; so consult with your local supply shop or emulsion manufacturer, or check on the Internet to determine a starting range of exposure time. Use the results for the exposure time of your final screen later.

For the test, you can use your design positive or a special exposure calculator, available from screen-printing supply shops. Follow the manufacturer's instructions for using the exposure calculator, or if you are using your design positive, cover most of the image with an opaque piece of paper. At equal time intervals, such as 10, 30, or 60 seconds, move the paper down to uncover more of the design. Jot down how much exposure each

area received. Immediately after the exposure, remove the design positive. Avoiding further exposure to light, move the screen to a tub and wash the screen with a power washer or strong nozzle attached to a hose. Unexposed areas should wash out cleanly, while the exposed areas remain. Too much washout (or *delamination*) usually means that you underexposed the area, used old emulsion, did not degrease the screen properly, or that the emulsion was layered too thickly. Not enough washout means overexposure at some point in the process. A perfectly exposed screen has complete washout in the printing areas, sharp edges to the motifs, and no washout in nonprinting areas. However, the latter issue can sometimes be fixed with a blockout pen or by applying a small amount of emulsion with a paintbrush, and then drying and re-exposing the screen.

Fabric Choice and Preparation

Prepared-for-dye (PFD) and prepared-for-printing (PFP) fabrics are the ideal choice for home printing. They are free of sizing and other processing agents that decrease the ink's binding agents from adhering to the fabric surface. Start your printing adventures with a smooth, tightly woven, nonstretch, medium- to heavyweight cellulose fiber fabric, such as cotton, linen, hemp, or a blend of these.

Predyed or preprinted fabric can also be used for printing, but keep in mind that inks vary in opacity and the base color will probably affect the ink colors. Prewashing on hot with mild laundry soap is recommended no matter what kind of base cloth you're using; even PFD/PFP fabrics pick up dirt and oils on their journey to you, and this soiling can affect print quality. Always test-print, cure, and launder on your base cloth of choice before attempting longer print runs.

For more about fabrics, see Know Your Surface: Fabric Basics (page 98).

BURN THE SCREEN

Prepare and then expose your final screen for the amount of time indicated by the results of the test exposure. After you wash it out and it is dry, inspect the screen against backlighting, covering any pinholes within the opaque design areas with blockout fluid or emulsion (remember to re-expose the screen if you do this).

Remove test photo emulsion stencils and failed stencils with screen reclaimer solvent, following the manufacturer's safety and disposal recommendations (also see Environmental and Safety Considerations, page 130).

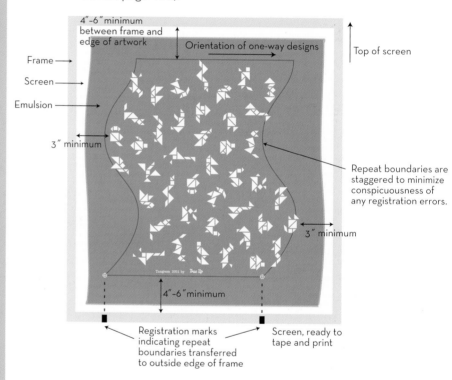

4"-6" minimum between frame and edge of artwork

Orientation of one-way designs

Top of screen

Frame

Screen

Emulsion

3" minimum

Repeat boundaries are staggered to minimize conspicuousness of any registration errors.

3" minimum

4"-6" minimum

Registration marks indicating repeat boundaries transferred to outside edge of frame

Screen, ready to tape and print

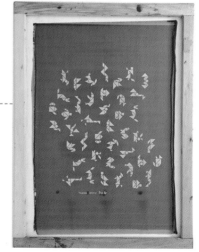

The exposed screen, ready to tape and print. Note orientation of the design to the screen.

Printing

Setup

1. Using screen tape, cover the edges of the screen on the squeegee/well side that are not filled with hardened emulsion. With the metal T-square, make lines on the outer edge of the frame on the side corresponding with the fabric selvage, aligned with the registration marks indicating your repeat.

Taping the screen

Taping completed

Transfer registration marks to screen frame.

TIP

Test your screen, ink, and squeegee skills by printing first onto inexpensive paper. Once you can achieve a consistent print, do a test repeat run on fabric, using inexpensive muslin.

2. Again using the T-square, measure from the edge of the frame to the edge of the print. This measurement determines where on the table you will place the edge of the fabric. Place pieces of masking tape along the length of the table this distance away from the top edge of the printing surface ruler. The fabric selvage will be aligned along the masking tape.

Measure from frame edge to print edge.

Measure from the top edge of the printing surface ruler to determine where to lay the edge of the fabric, and place tape.

3. Spread the fabric onto the printing surface. To determine where you will be placing the screen for printing each repeat, multiply the repeat height by 2, 3, 4, 5, and so forth. Jot down where your repeat boundaries will lie. For example, for my 16″ repeat:

Repeat #	Left registration mark	Right registration mark
1	0	16
2	16	32
3	32	48
4	48	64
5	64	80

4. Lay the uninked screen onto the fabric where you will be printing your first repeat. Using the T-pins, secure the fabric to the print surface just outside the edges of the screen frame. Repeat at the remaining odd-numbered repeats. This will keep the fabric from lifting and distorting when you lift the screen after printing.

Pinning fabric to surface

Printing Procedure

1. If desired, mix your ink with retarder according to the manufacturer's instructions. This will help prevent the water-based ink from drying in the screen, which can ruin both your print and your screen.

2. For the first print only, you must first *flood* the screen, meaning you push ink into the printing areas while the screen is raised off the substrate. Prop up one edge of the screen with a clean jar or block. (Don't be tempted to use your drippy ink jar!) Pour a line of ink above the printing area. Allow a few inches of space for the ink to sit between the resting squeegee and the top of the printing area. Pull the ink across the screen with the squeegee at a 60° angle. Push the ink back to the top of the screen.

Flood the screen.

Flooding the screen—pushing ink back up to top of screen

3. Have a partner remove the prop and hold the top of the screen off the fabric as you align the registration marks on the screen frame according to the measurements you determined in Setup, Step 2 (previous page). When the screen is properly aligned, have your partner gently lay the screen down on the fabric.

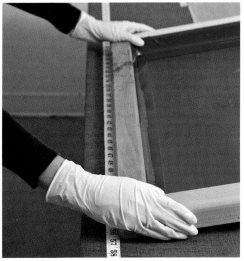

Partner holds up top edge of screen while you align the registration marks.

4. Test a print on paper lying atop the fabric first. Print the first repeat by pulling ink over the screen with the squeegee at a 60° angle and then pushing ink back to the top of the screen (see diagrams below). You will likely need to make 2 or 3 printing passes for a clear print. It takes practice to get this procedure down with even squeegee pressure, speed, and ink coverage. Make sure you get consistent prints on paper before moving to fabric.

5. Print the odd-numbered repeats down the entire length of your fabric, each time having your partner hold the top edge of the screen up while you align the marks at the bottom. You must allow ink to dry to the touch on the fabric before printing the even-numbered repeats. Unfortunately, this creates the danger of the ink drying in the screen. Using retarder and flooding the screen (Step 2, page 127) between sessions will prevent the screen from drying. Whenever you pause a printing session, make a test print on paper before resuming printing on your "good" fabric. If the ink is not passing through the screen well—you can tell because your print will be light and blotchy—wash out the screen immediately with water and let it dry before resuming. Also, prior to printing the even-numbered repeats, repeat Setup, Step 4 (page 126), moving the T-pins to secure the fabric to the printing surface.

Printing repeats. Fabric was relocated to show all odd-numbered repeats in photo.

Printing repeats in action

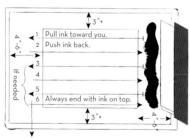

LAST: Lift and move screen to next alternating repeat.

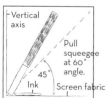

The print procedure (post–screen flood) and squeegee angle

A FIELD GUIDE TO FABRIC DESIGN

Finished fabric

Cleanup and Curing

Use a spatula to scoop unused ink from the screen back into its jar. Thoroughly wash the screen (remove screen tape as you go), the squeegee, and the spatula with water (and a diluted cleaning agent, if recommended by the ink manufacturer).

After air drying, water-based inks require heat setting to cure. The manufacturer usually specifies the time and temperature needed (look for technical specs on the manufacturer's website if not included with the ink). For home printing, curing can be achieved by ironing (always use a pressing cloth) or tumble drying. Heat set when the ink is no longer tacky to the touch.

Advanced Techniques

Screen printing full-width fabrics is almost the same process as the one outlined in this section, only on a larger scale. Screens that cover the entire fabric width are expensive and unwieldy, but you can use smaller screens with designs that repeat on all four edges and print widthwise as well as lengthwise. Or forego repeats altogether and print a mock tossed print with individual motifs. Either way, be careful not to lay the screen in wet ink.

For full-width printing, two people (or one very tall person) are needed to pull the squeegee across the screen, which takes practice to achieve an even print. Professional hand-screen-printing tables can run the entire length of their warehouses or studios. These are typically outfitted with a rail and adjustable stoppers, which are preset to move the screen quickly down the fabric length.

For multicolor printing, you must create separate screens for each color and register them both in the exact same place on their screens, both horizontally and vertically. Use registration marks liberally and cover up marks you don't want printed postexposure. Print light to dark. When setting up positives for the bottom color or colors, grow or trap (slightly enlarging all around) the color areas that underlie subsequent printing layers so that registration is a little more forgiving. Remember: Never lay your screen onto wet ink!

TIP

Cut the usable portions of "mistake" pieces and use them in scrappy projects or sell in remnant packs.

129

All About Inks

Screen printing onto fabric yardage is usually done with water-based pigment inks. Manufacturers' stock ink colors are typically quite limited. You can mix your own freestyle (a color wheel is handy here), order Pantone-color-matched premixed inks (for a premium), or mix your own according to a formula guide. The latter is great if you are printing fabric to sell and want to keep the ink color as consistent as possible.

The Pantone Formula Guide for solid uncoated inks (on paper) provides ink formulas listed in parts: for example, 10 parts Pantone Yellow, 6 parts Pantone Process Blue, ½ part Pantone Black. (For more about the Pantone systems, see Using the Pantone Matching System, page 68.) Use a good-quality digital scale with a *tare* feature, which resets the display to zero with weight already on the scale, and multiple measuring unit modes. Place your mixing container on the scale; zero out (tare); add the specified amount of one color; zero out again; add the specified amount of the next color; zero out—continue until all the colors are added, and then mix thoroughly and label the container. Matsui offers water-based inks in basic Pantone colors and free ink-mixing software. The software calculates formulas for Pantone colors using these base inks, based on how much total ink you want to make. No matter which Pantone guide you work with, you can cross-reference colors using myPantone X-Ref, available for use free online (see Resources, page 158).

Beyond Pigment Ink

Water-based pigment inks are most commonly used for textile screen printing, but they limit you to using light-colored fabrics. Alternatives include the following:

Discharge inks bleach out the background color of darker fabrics and can be used on their own or as a base for overprinting.

Thickened reactive dyes yield a softer hand to the fabric and are more wash-fast than water-based inks because they become part of the fabric's structure. Just be aware that the dye-setting process adds extra steps to an already labor-intensive process.

Novelty inks—fluorescents, metallics, glitter—add pizzazz to your printing. They are available in water-based and plastisol formulations.

Plastisol inks are easier than water-based inks to print with and cure, but they have a noticeable hand, emit unpleasant volatile organic compounds (VOCs), and require solvents for cleanup. For these reasons, they're not typically used for printing fabric yardage.

Environmental and Safety Considerations

Use biodegradable, noncaustic, and nontoxic inks, screen cleaners, reclaimers, and degreasers whenever possible.

The water-based inks used for fabric printing get fairly high marks in terms of safety and environmental friendliness. They clean up with water, but they might contain other solvents and pigments that make washing them down the drain irresponsible. Inquire with the retailer or manufacturer to choose drain-safe inks.

Conventional reclaiming solvents, which are sprayed on a stencil to remove stencils from the screen, are very toxic, so wear gloves, a respirator, and goggles when using these solvents. Contact local screen-printing shops to see if they offer a screen reclaiming service. Let them worry about safety equipment and proper wastewater disposal so you don't have to.

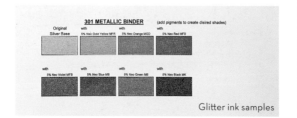

Glitter ink samples

Creating a Work Surface

Work surfaces for hand printing fabric are easy and inexpensive to build from materials available from home improvement stores. These surfaces are padded so that the ink or dye can better penetrate the fabric—the cloth surface also helps prevent the base cloth from slipping.

For block printing, your work surface needs only to be the width of the fabric plus a few inches, but even that's not critical. You can use a smaller surface and move the fabric around as you work.

If the surface will be primarily used for screen printing, build the widest and longest work surface you can fit into your space with enough room to maneuver around it comfortably. The chart below will help you determine the minimum screen *height* you need to print the entire width of the

fabric. To determine the screen *width* you need, add at least 6″ to your design (for 3″ of clearance to the left and right of the squeegee) *plus* 3″ for the frame for *a total of 9″*. (Check with your supplier for exact frame profile measurements.)

Then, to determine the *table width* you need, find the fabric width you plan on printing most in the left-hand column of the chart, and add at least 6″ to the Screen + Frame measurement listed in the third column (or use the standard screen sizes in the fourth column if you think you'll be limited to stock sizes from screen-printing supply houses). Build the table as long as is feasible for your space—the longer the table, the longer the length of fabric you will be able to print at a time.

SCREEN-PRINTING REFERENCE CHART—SCREEN SIZES

Fabric width	Minimum internal screen height (4″ minimum clearance above and below design, for a total of 8″)	Screen + frame height measurement, or external screen dimensions (assuming 1½″-wide frame)	Closest standard screen sizes
22″ (half width of 44″–45″-wide fabric for printing fat quarters)	30″	33″	36″ × 25″ *†, 36″ × 36″ †
27″ (half width of 54″–55″-wide fabric)	35″	38″	40″ × 30″ †
30″ (half width of 60″-wide fabric)	38″	41″	48″ × 36″ †
36″	44″	47″	48″ × 36″ †
45″	53″	56″	72″ × 48″ †
54″	62″	65″	72″ × 48″ †
60″	68″	71″	72″ × 48″ †
Custom (p)	p + 8″	p + 11″	n/a

*From Pocono Mountain Screen Supply
†From Victory Factory
Note: Pocono Mountain Screen Supply also offers custom-sized frames up to 60″ × 60″ (see Resources, page 158).

- 1 sheet of 4' × 8' × ½" hardwood plywood (lighter) or MDF (heavier/sturdier)

- 2 premium-grade 2" × 4" × 38" fir planks

- 2 premium-grade 2" × 4" × 27" fir planks

- 10' length of pine or hardwood 2" × 3"

- 6' × 9' roll of carpet padding, or 2 layers of synthetic quilt batting, each covering a 4" × 8" area plus extra to staple underneath, or 2–3 layers of 72"-wide acrylic craft felt (about 6 yards for 2 layers or 9 yards for 3 layers)

- 45"- or 60"-wide tightly woven, smooth canvas*

- Cloth tape measure

- Hot glue

- Power saw, unless wood is cut to size at the store

- Hammer

- Nail gun (optional but nice)

- 16d 3½" nails

- 18-gauge finishing nails

- Sandpaper

- T-square

- Level

- Measuring tape

- Pencil

- Titebond glue

- Staple gun and staples

If using sawhorses as temporary table legs:

- 4 sawhorse brackets (to make 2 sawhorses)

- 3 premium-grade 2" × 4"s, cut into 8 pieces 28" each for sawhorse legs

- 6d 2" common nails

If you're building a wider table, rosebrand.com supplies wider-width canvas by the yard.

Basic Table

The plans provided here show how to build a 40"-wide × 8'-long surface for printing 22"-wide fabric, unattached to legs so that you can flip the surface on its side for storage (but never do that alone—this tabletop is quite heavy). If you are lucky enough to have a dedicated space for printing, it's preferable to affix table legs permanently for stability.

Assemble the frame with a hammer and 16d 3½" nails according to the illustration. Ensure all joins are 90°. Using the Titebond glue, adhere the 40" × 96" plywood sheet to the frame according to the diagram below, and then secure with finishing nails. Ensure that the surface is level. Lightly sand edges and nail holes.

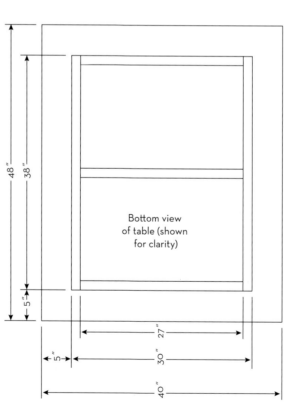

Bottom view of table (shown for clarity)

Plans for printing surface

Stretch layers of padding (felt, batting, or carpet pad) over the table surface and tack into place with a staple gun. Double-check that the padding is smooth and taut. Along with a partner, flip the table surface over, staple the padding down completely to the underside of the plywood, and trim the excess. Snip fabric from the corners of the padding to reduce the bulk when stapling the corners down. Flip the surface back over, and repeat the process with the canvas layer.

Assemble 2 sawhorses, set the table surface on top of them, and gently shake the table to make sure it is reasonably sturdy (there will be some give). Adhere the cloth tape measure to one long edge of the tabletop with the glue gun, ensuring it is perfectly straight.

(Bigger) finished printing surface with affixed tape measure

DESIGNER ROUNDTABLE:
Why Do You Screen-Print?

Why did you choose hand screen-printing? What about it appeals to you among the other options? What are the drawbacks?

It is such a satisfying medium, with an immediacy and tactile quality that sending our designs to someone else to print wouldn't have for us. There are usually minimum quantities that you have to order when having fabric printed commercially, and doing it ourselves allows us to keep our production run small and change things as often as we like. Also, it is tremendously fun.

—AROUNNA KHOUNNORAJ AND ROISIN FAGAN

I started out screen printing everything by hand myself, and then handed over the job to someone with much stronger hands and shoulders! I like the idea of each print being squeezed out by a pair of hands, but I've found the failure rate of hand screen-printing very high. The romance of it doesn't justify wasting fabric on unusable prints, so I've switched to rotary printing. Both ecologically and economically, rotary makes more sense. —HEATHER MOORE

We are a bunch of battlers really, and like doing things the hard way! You can screen-print on a small scale or right up to quite a large scale, so it is very adaptable for growth without a huge outlay. There isn't a lot of industry in Australia for other types of printing. We love machines too, but handmade has a quality more directly suited to represent our work as artists. We love layering and customizing colors, which is not possible with large-scale production.

—AMY PRIOR AND CARLY SCHWERDT

133

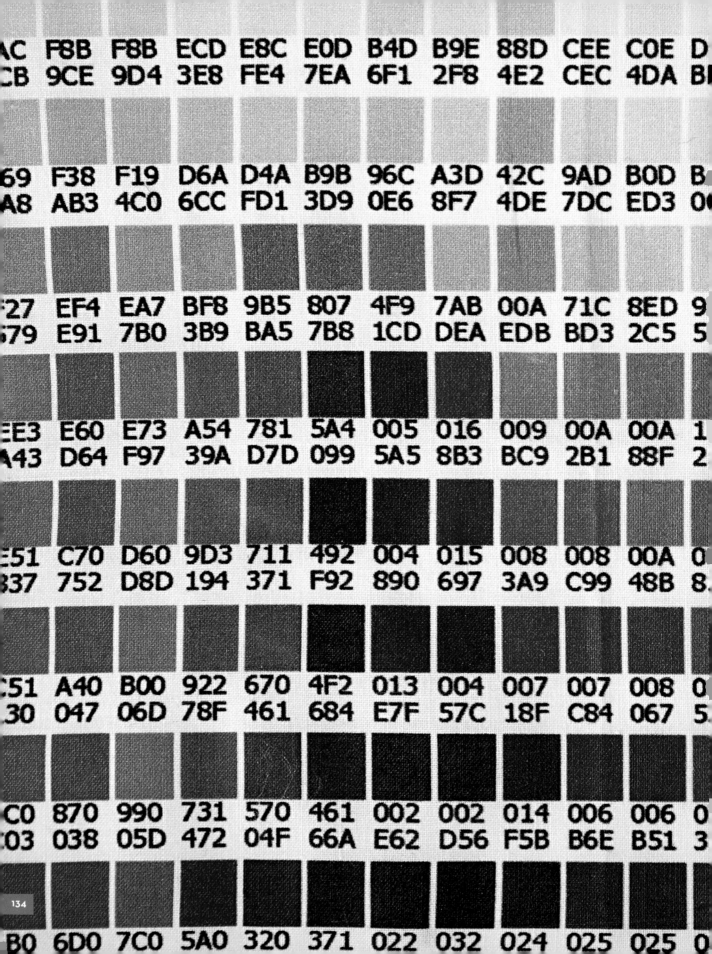

AC F8B F8B ECD E8C E0D B4D B9E 88D CEE C0E D
CB 9CE 9D4 3E8 FE4 7EA 6F1 2F8 4E2 CEC 4DA B

69 F38 F19 D6A D4A B9B 96C A3D 42C 9AD B0D B
A8 AB3 4C0 6CC FD1 3D9 0E6 8F7 4DE 7DC ED3 00

27 EF4 EA7 BF8 9B5 807 4F9 7AB 00A 71C 8ED 9
79 E91 7B0 3B9 BA5 7B8 1CD DEA EDB BD3 2C5 5

EE3 E60 E73 A54 781 5A4 005 016 009 00A 00A 1
A43 D64 F97 39A D7D 099 5A5 8B3 BC9 2B1 88F 2

51 C70 D60 9D3 711 492 004 015 008 008 00A 0
37 752 D8D 194 371 F92 890 697 3A9 C99 48B 8

51 A40 B00 922 670 4F2 013 004 007 007 008 0
30 047 06D 78F 461 684 E7F 57C 18F C84 067 5

C0 870 990 731 570 461 002 002 014 006 006 0
03 038 05D 472 04F 66A E62 D56 F5B B6E B51 3

B0 6D0 7C0 5A0 320 371 022 032 024 025 025

Digital Printing

In digital textile printing, fabric is fed from a roll through a large-format inkjet printer—basically a supersized version of the familiar desktop printer. The technology has been around for more than a decade—mostly in print bureaus that serve the textile and fashion industries. Recently, however, it has become accessible to and affordable for independent and amateur designers, thanks to lower-cost bureaus geared mainly toward hobbyists and cottage industrialists.

The technology is completely changing the face of the textile and fashion industries. Traditional volume printing methods require several weeks to months, and hundreds of dollars at a minimum, just to produce strike-offs (test prints). Going into production requires several more months and minimum purchases of 1,000–3,000 yards. In contrast, digital textile printing allows yardage to be printed instantly, so manufacturers can bring sample products to market at a much faster pace.

Because of the costs and volume involved in traditional printing, a fabric manufacturer must be certain that designs are commercially viable. The need to appeal to the masses discourages experimentation. Now, with digital printing, anyone can print any design he or she desires. For the designer producing retail fabrics, the print-on-demand aspect is a boon; the only thing lost when a design fails is the time and relatively modest expense it took to create the design.

Digital printing also lifts the constraints of repeats and limited color. The size of a digital fabric design is limited only by the width of the fabric, but it could theoretically span endlessly along the length of the fabric (of course, this would require a large file, which at some point would overload the processing capabilities of the computer running the printer software). Gone are screen setup fees and spot colors; digital printers can produce millions of colors as easily as they can two or three. Digital textile printing also happens to be significantly more eco-friendly than traditional methods—there is very little waste ink or dye.

While turnaround is relatively fast, the actual printing speed of most digital printers is painfully slow. These machines produce fewer than 20 yards per hour (usually fewer than 10), compared with traditional rotary or roller machines, which print hundreds or even thousands of yards per hour. Faster digital printers are on the market but are, of course, significantly more expensive. Partially due to speed, and partially due to equipment, supplies, and labor costs, digital printing also remains relatively costly for the consumer or cottage industrialist wishing to produce his or her own fabric for sale. These problems are likely to diminish, however, as the technology evolves over the next couple of decades.

Digital printing uses special software to print the basic design as a square, half-drop, brick, or other repeat type and to control color. Other than that, it's not much more mysterious than your average desktop printer. However, different digital print bureaus work with either water-based pigment ink printing, dye printing, or a process called dye sublimation—sometimes all three—and it's important to know the difference.

Detail from Spoonflower color chart (page 68)

Pigment, Dye, and Dye Sublimation Printing

Digital textile printers can print with water-based pigment inks, with dyes, or by using dye sublimation methods. A summary of each method follows.

Medium-weight cotton with water-based pigment ink

Medium-weight cotton with reactive dyes

Polyester satin with dye sublimation

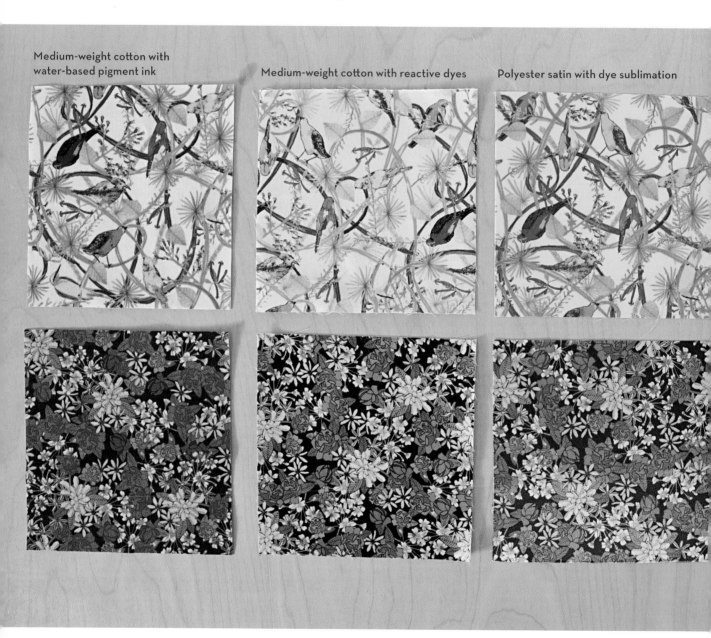

A FIELD GUIDE TO FABRIC DESIGN

Water-based pigment inks use binders to adhere to the surface of the fiber. The cost of the inks is comparable to that of dyes, but the base cloths do not require pretreatment and the inks cure with heat, so the process is less costly overall and low-impact environmentally. Dark, saturated colors are difficult to achieve, and adjacent areas of similar dark colors may turn out with insufficient contrast. These inks can fade if the binding agent breaks down because of light, abrasion, or laundering. To preserve color in pigment-printed fabrics, use a mild, phosphate-free detergent or dry-clean them.

Reactive or acid dyes can also be used by digital printers. Reactive dyes are used mainly for cellulose fibers (cotton and linen), nylon, and protein fibers (silk and wool); acid dyes are mainly used for protein fibers (silk and wool) and nylon. Dyes can achieve brighter, more saturated color than pigment inks (especially with dark colors) and are more colorfast because the dye molecules become part of the fiber's structure. Fabrics must be pretreated so that they are receptive to dye, and once printed the dyes must be steam set and then laundered. Pretreatment chemicals, energy consumption, and wastewater from laundering make digital printing with dyes less environmentally friendly than pigment printing. However, reactive dyes are nontoxic, and very little dye ends up in the wastewater—only a tiny fraction of effluent compared with that of traditional rotary-printing (and even hand screen-printing) methods.

Dye sublimation printing is a process reserved for synthetic fabrics. The design is printed onto a roll of specialized transfer paper, which is then transferred to the surface of the fabric with heat. It is similar to T-shirt iron-ons, except it is a large-format, continuous process. Dye sublimation printing can achieve very bold, bright colors and fine detail.

Two prints by British designer Lydia Meiying, each printed with the three basic digital printing processes. Medium-weight cotton with water-based pigment ink (*left*), medium-weight cotton with reactive dyes (*center*), and polyester satin with dye sublimation (*right*). The reactive dye print is the sharpest of the three. The colors are also the most saturated, especially noticeable with the dark background color.

Digital Printing Services

Currently there are hundreds of digital textile printing bureaus worldwide, but only a handful are priced for use by hobbyists and small-scale fabric producers (as opposed to textile and fashion industry professionals). Higher-end printers provide a lot more one-on-one guidance, as well as fine-tuning of design and colors. They typically use reactive dyes, which are more vibrant and durable than pigment inks. Hobby-oriented printing services such as Spoonflower rely on volume, so they print your files with little or no intervention or modification on their end. They are geared toward customers who are tech-savvy enough to prepare their digital files for optimal printing results on their own, and who consider the lack of hand-holding an excellent trade-off for the lower prices. They also tend to use pigment inks, which involve less equipment and labor. However, a few hobby-oriented printing services offer reactive dye printing.

All bureaus can print your digital file unrepeated or as a square, half-drop, brick, or mirrored repeat. You upload a tile—the repeat contained in a rectangle. (Note that you still have to set up the design file so that it will flow as your repeat of choice; the printer's software will not do that for you.)

When choosing a digital printing service, first consider the fabric on which you wish to print, and shop around to see which services offer it.

If you prefer reactive dye printing, your choices are further restricted. Whether you choose pigment printing or dyes, make sure the bureau stands by the colorfastness of its products and will reprint fabrics or provide a refund if your fabric fades significantly. I have had positive experiences with all the bureaus listed in the Resources section (see Digital Textile Print Bureaus, page 159). Finally, ask about their current turnaround times if you're working on a deadline.

Color in Digital Printing

In Know Your Color (page 59), you learned about the challenge of matching colors from hand-rendered or digitally created designs to inks or dyes printed on fabric. If you're printing fabric with one of the affordable digital printing services, you alone are responsible for setting up the colors in your design.

If color fidelity is important to you, it's vital that you reference physical color standards in the digital setup of your pattern. Due to variations between bureaus and how different base cloths absorb the ink or dye, the only reliable standard is a color chart (sometimes called a color blanket) from the print bureau with which you intend to do business, printed onto their base cloth of your choice. To be useful to you in the design process, the colors will be labeled with codes. The colors might be derived from a well-known color space (RGB/Hex, CMYK, CIELAB) supported by a popular image editing program of choice, or they might be from the printer's own system, in which case a digital color-space file is also supplied. You simply pick your desired colors from the color blanket, input the code into your program's color picker, and fill the colors into your design. As you learned in Color Models, page 67, the color gamut of any of these commonly used color spaces is quite different from that of the system used by digital printers, but that is irrelevant in this case. As long as you have the physical standards, you know how the color on-screen will look printed onto fabric.

However, even if you have set up the file properly using the color blanket, you still have not seen the colors applied to your design and printed onto fabric. Keep in mind that the color blanket contains little squares of color, all equal in size to one another. The proportion of colors in your design and their proximity to one another affect the final outcome. Even if they looked fine on-screen, your chosen colors might not work exactly as you expected on fabric. That's why it's also vital to print a swatch of your design to do a final color check before you commit to yardage. This costs a bit of time and money, but it's a small price to pay compared with the price of yardage that you can't use.

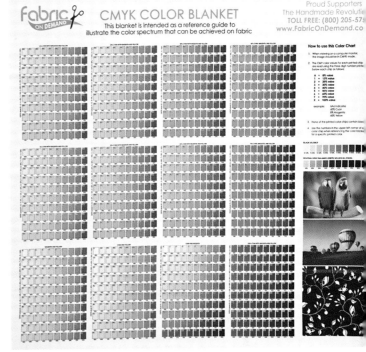

Color chart from Fabric on Demand digital textile printing service

Quality Control with Digitally Printed Fabrics

Though all reputable printers inspect their fabrics before shipping, occasionally someone might miss an off-grain or blurry print, so be sure to do your own inspection upon your fabric's arrival so that errors can be resolved immediately.

First, check the entire length of the fabric for stray blotches or marks. Next, if you sent your file in at the recommended dpi, the print should appear sharp and well defined. Finally, check that the print is on-grain. Eyeball how the print is oriented relative to the selvage. If you're still not sure, you can try ripping woven fabrics widthwise (selvage to selvage). The rip will be true to the cross-grain. Some fabrics can be ripped lengthwise too. A more gentle method is to clip into the selvage, then grab a weft yarn or two and pull them out. This will create a noticeable, on-grain guideline. Is the print significantly skewed relative to the line or edge? If so, return your fabric for a refund or replacement.

DESIGNER ROUNDTABLE:
Why Digital?

Why did you decide on printing digitally instead of hand printing or licensing your designs?

The opportunity to license my designs has not come up yet, but if it did, I would definitely look into it. I do love the digital printing because it is a very quick process and you are in control of all the decisions. —HEIDI KENNEY

I decided to go with digital printing because of the low startup costs and the practically limitless color palette. I'd love to license my future collections, but for now I'm really enjoying producing my own fabric because of the freedom I have to make changes. —JASONDA DESMOND

I would love to have the time and equipment to hand print, although the convenience of digital printing allows me to create images almost instantly (without the mess and lack of space to screen print!). Spoonflower is a great source for surface designers to get started, whether it's for personal use or to be recognized in the industry. This is another reason I chose digital design— the images can be uploaded and tweaked, if needed, in an instant. —ALICE BURROWS

Have you been happy with the color saturation and wash-fastness?

The saturation is so important to me, because I love to use bright, contrasting colorways. So far I have been really satisfied with the results, and I always get so excited by adding new designs and waiting to see the results on fabric. —ALICE BURROWS

Sometimes the colors can be a challenge, most especially for me because a lot of my designs are made using scanned cut paper. It is not as easy to control the colors. Mostly I have been happy. —HEIDI KENNEY

My first collection was designed to work with the limitations of digital printing right from the beginning. I was especially concerned that the colors would not come out correctly, so I was careful to create the designs so that they could easily be changed. Luckily, they came out perfectly and I couldn't be happier. The wash-fastness has been great. I wouldn't hesitate to use digitally printed fabric for any project. —JASONDA DESMOND

THE WORLD OF FABRIC DESIGN

Designing for Fun

Designing as a Business

Meet the Roundtable Designers

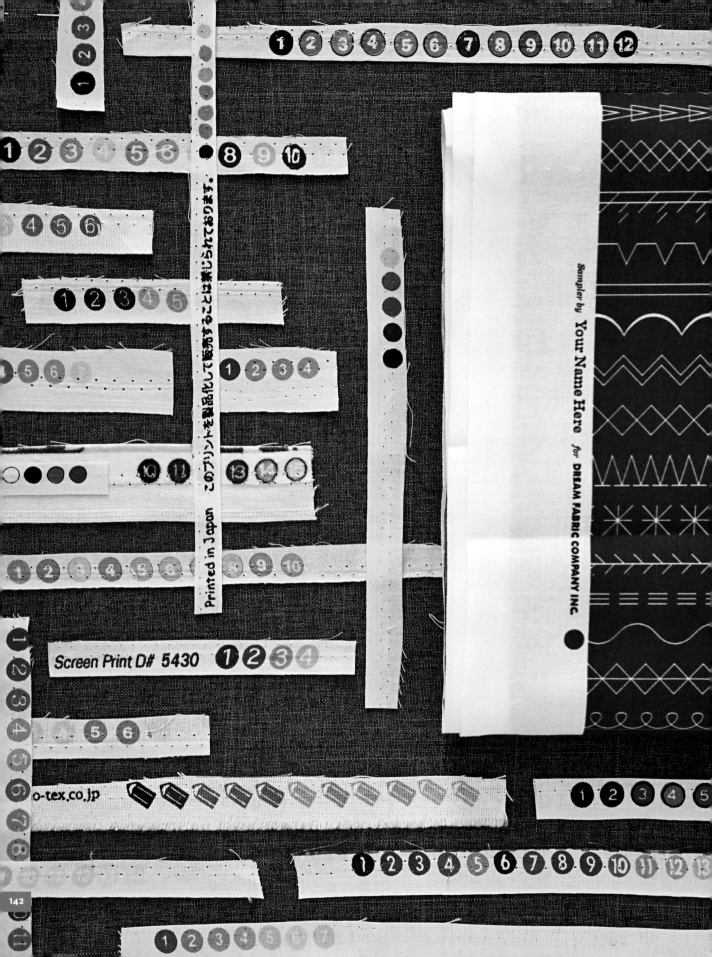

Printed in Japan このプリントを製品化して販売することは禁じられております。

Sampler by *Your Name Here* for **DREAM FABRIC COMPANY INC.**

Screen Print D# 5430

o-tex.co.jp

Designing for Fun and Profit

Do you want to design and print textiles as a hobby or as a business venture? This chapter will explore these different routes so you can decide which is the best for you.

Short-Run Designing for Fun

Fabric design *is* fun, so there's nothing wrong with wanting to do it just for kicks. The volume fabric printing processes that I'm personally most interested in result in a consistent product, and a lot of it. Therefore, they're usually more suited for business. But block printing is very affordable; screen printing *can* be; and digital printing, while not exactly cheap, requires no setup costs if you already have a computer. These short-run printing processes are described in Step-by-Step Hand Printing (page 111) and Digital Printing (page 135).

If you simply wish to embellish small pieces of fabric up to a few yards, consider low-tech methods like direct painting or drawing on fabric, stencils and stamps, or inkjet transfers. These methods are even less costly than block and screen printing, and they require few to no specialized supplies. My favorite books that demonstrate these methods are listed in Resources (page 158). Here, I've listed some project ideas that might launch your first short-run printing adventure.

Gifts. Make tea towels, pillows, dolls—for the whole family, a class at school, or your colleagues at work. Incorporate kids' artwork for a wonderful keepsake.

Custom textiles for the home. When nothing commercial will do, print your own fabric for upholstering furniture or for curtains, pillows, tea towels, bedsheets, placemats, coasters, napkins, duvet covers, room dividers, or lampshades.

Clothing. Build a whole wardrobe from the fabric print of your dreams.

Costumes. Your kid wants to be a Sleestak for Halloween, but your local fabric shop is fresh out of snakeskin-print Lycra. Print your own instead!

Wedding textiles. Customize tablecloths, napkins, handkerchiefs, table runners, place cards, and favors with the couple's names, wedding date, and other thematic elements.

Team builders. Think beyond the T-shirt— make fabric for scarves, PJ pants, or tote bags for family reunions, summer campers, and community groups.

Promotions. Make unforgettable promotional items using your small business logo.

Attention getters. Print your own banners, flags, or signs for a cause, a show, or a sale.

Art. Incorporate custom-printed fabric into quilts and other textiles or mixed-media work.

Designing for Profit

Self-production and licensing are the two main routes to consider if you want to design fabric to sell. Each has its advantages, disadvantages, and best-suited production methods.

As enthusiastic as I am about designing fabric for the retail market, I have to state a major disclaimer up front: It's not a big-money venture. Unless you are a full-time textile designer for a company, *it is very rare to live off retail fabric design alone.* I've heard designers say over and over that they do what they do because they love it, not because it pays all the bills. The good news is, you can have a full-time creative career in the fabric business, or at least get closer to it, by building your brand and selling other related products.

Self-Production

Being both a designer and a producer of fabric is an increasingly popular route. No matter which production method you use, you enjoy full control over your designs and can work on your own timetables. The most accessible printing methods—hand printing and digital printing—are best for short runs, which in turn allow you to be more experimental and forward-thinking with your designs. An example is small South African producer Shine Shine, which produces whimsical, artistic fabrics inspired by African commemorative cloths.

But with control comes responsibility. You not only have to have your hands in—and pay for—every aspect of production, but you are also responsible for marketing, shipping, bookkeeping, and all the other less-than-thrilling aspects of running a business.

That doesn't faze you? Then the only thing to decide is what you're going to print, how you're going to print it, and how you're going to sell it.

Jackie So by Heidi Chisholm for Shine Shine

The how-tos of designing and printing are covered earlier in this book, but the table Choosing a Printing Method (page 146) will help you decide which printing method to pursue based on startup and production costs, the types of designs you're envisioning, and other factors.

144

Volume Printing Methods

Traditionally, fabric is printed in mills using one of three basic methods: automated flatbed screen printing, rotary screen printing, or copper roller printing.

Automated flatbed screen printing uses flat screens just like those used for screen printing by hand. A stencil is chemically adhered to a fine mesh, and the print paste (containing pigment or dye) is pressed through it and onto the fabric. Because the process is controlled by machine, it is far more efficient than screen printing by hand. Automated flatbed printing allows larger repeats (up to 24" high), but fewer colors than rotary screen printing. It is economical for shorter print runs. The design repeats can be any size that is evenly divisible into the main measurement of the screen.

In **rotary screen printing,** the screens are rolled into the form of a cylinder, and the print paste is fed to the inside of the roller and pressed onto the fabric, which is fed continuously underneath. Most rollers are 25¼" in circumference, so that is the maximum height of the repeat. Rollers range in width and can be used to print very wide goods. Some printing equipment can accommodate dozens of colors, but most are more limited. Minimum orders for rotary screen printing typically start at 1,000–3,000 yards per design.

Copper roller printing used to be commonplace but now represents only a small fraction of the textiles printed today. It is a form of intaglio printing that allows for extremely fine detail, but prints smaller repeats. It allows fewer colors than rotary printing. The rollers are expensive and the etching requires skilled artisans, so minimums are very high.

For all three methods, each color in the design requires a separate screen or roller, and each additional color means additional expense. If you work directly with a mill or license your designs to a converter (a fabric manufacturer), they will let you know what kind of equipment they work with and the repeat and color specs you must follow. If you're creating designs in anticipation of volume printing but don't have specifics, just keep in mind that screens and rollers require you to keep areas of color consistent between colorways. For example, if a print with fruit has a red apple and a red strawberry, in most cases you can't make the strawberry blue and the apple green in a second colorway.

Another thing to keep in mind is that multicolor prints are usually built up from lightest to darkest colors. In a process called trapping, areas of underlying, lighter colors that abut other darker colors (such as the fill color of an outlined flower) are enlarged slightly. If there are errors in registration, trapping minimizes or eliminates gaps. So if the background is the lightest color in your design, as a general rule, it must also be the lightest color in your other colorways.

Choosing a Printing Method

	Startup cost	# of colors	Maximum repeat size	Minimum yardage	Turnaround time	Cost per yard (cloth + printing) after setup costs
Block printing	< $50	Theoretically unlimited, but consider registration difficulties and expense of additional blocks/screens	Premounted blocks available up to 24″ × 36″, but unmounted rubber or lino can be cut and mounted to larger base	None	1 week	$2 and up
Hand screen printing	$100–$500		A few feet, but bigger screens get unwieldy and expensive			
Digital printing	< $50 with puchase of a color chart; cost of computer/ design software not included	Unlimited	Limited only by file size constraints	None	1–4 weeks	$16–$80 depending on base cloth; some bureaus offer quantity discounts
Mass production: flatbed or rotary screen printing	Can be several hundred dollars for screen setup fees and strikeoffs.	8–26 colors, depending on mill capabilities	Usually 24″ or 25¼″	Typically 1,000–3,000 yards but some converters have lower minimums	6+ months	Starting around $2 for short runs from over-seas sources; depends highly on base cloth fiber, quality, # of colors. Costs double to qua-druple if choosing domestic and/ or organic base cloth and printing methods. Shipping and cus-toms charges can also double costs at low volumes.

Outsourcing Production

Most individuals, especially if coming from outside the textile industry, will find it a huge challenge to source volume printing services (also called *textile converters*), especially if you wish to produce short runs of 1,000 yards or less per print. And even if you can establish a source, it's a huge undertaking to go this route.

Most textile print production is done in Asia. While it's getting easier to find converters online, it's difficult to know whether they are reputable. (Always ask for references.)

Just a handful of textile printing mills are left in the United States, but domestic printing often means higher minimums and cost per yard. Still, there are a myriad of reasons—economic, environmental, ethical—to choose domestic over foreign production, and there is a small (but hopefully growing) and loyal market that is willing to pay a premium for products "Made in America."

The best way to source converters is the old way—by word of mouth. Because this kind of information is so hard earned, though, it's highly unlikely that established designers and producers will share their sources with you. You're more

likely to burn a bridge than build one by asking. But consider this: Mass production requires that you have knowledge in everything from base cloth sourcing, to print design, to color correction, to finishes, to international shipping and customs. If you don't have that level of expertise, work to build it. And with it might come the business networking that could lead to printing sources. In the meantime, here are some other ways you might find a converter.

- Some U.S.-based quilting fabric manufacturers offer custom production runs (typically produced overseas), but minimums are typically 3,000 yards per print.

- Digital printers and hand screen printers might be willing and able to refer you to sources for larger print runs.

- Converters exhibit at the big textile and fashion trade shows, such as Magic, GlobalTex, Texworld, and Premiere Vision; but again, finding converters willing to print small minimums can be a challenge.

- Hand screen-printing services are easier to find, but be prepared for a much higher price bracket.

Selling Retail versus Wholesale

As a self-producer you will have to decide whether you want to sell wholesale, retail, or both. Retail prices are typically 400% of production costs (don't forget to include labor costs as well as materials), and it's natural to want to keep all that profit margin of 300% for yourself. But depending on how much fabric you have to move, it can take a significant amount of time and effort. Wholesale will typically only net 100% of your initial investment, but you are selling much larger quantities and can therefore recoup your investment and

start seeing a profit more quickly. Your retailers become a built-in marketing machine, increasing your brand recognition and, ideally, demand for your product. Some designers or producers want the best of both worlds, and they sell both wholesale and retail. Just be aware that some problems are inherent in making your customers your competition. If you do choose to sell both ways, the number one rule is never to undercut other retailers selling your product.

Licensing

If you are willing to trade a bit of control and profit to have someone else take on the burdens of production and marketing, then the world of licensing is for you. Large fabric companies like Robert Kaufman and FreeSpirit print fabric designs that are either produced in-house or licensed from freelance designers.

THE QUILTING FABRIC MARKET

The biggest segment of the retail fabric market is quilting cotton. Quilting is a huge industry. According to the Quilting in America 2010 survey, 16.38 million U.S. households have a quilter, and the average annual expenditure of the million or so "dedicated quilters" (those who spend $600+/year) is $2,442.

Fabric produced by big-name manufacturers is of very high quality, and this medium-weight, 100% cotton cloth is suitable for many applications other than quilting. In recent years, the industry has responded to the new generation of sewists interested in sewing apparel and other crafts. Now, alongside quilting cotton, it's not unusual to see collections in cotton voile, cotton lawn, rayon, polyester fleece, laminated cotton, and heavy home décor–weight canvas. (One trendsetting

company, Westminster Fibers, recently and appropriately rebranded itself from a quilting cotton to a "lifestyle fabrics" manufacturer.)

Licensing your designs to a large fabric company is an attractive route for several reasons. First and foremost, you get your name published as a designer, which is rare in the industry at large. Moreover, you have a company behind you to help fine-tune your collection so it has the best chance at being a hit. Some companies also take care of all the marketing. They pay for print and online advertising, hire people to design and sew samples, and foot the bill for you to attend and exhibit at the huge semiannual International Quilt Market. Other companies leave some or all of that up to you.

Sign you up? Well, a lot of others feel that way too. Kyle Sanchez of Robert Kaufman Fabrics reports that they receive approximately 20 portfolio submissions a week and that they've had to set up a dedicated department to process and review submissions. The company produces a couple of dozen collections per season, only a part of which are by new artists, so that gives you an idea of the competition.

SUBMITTING DESIGNS

How can you stand out in such a competitive area? It's helpful to have a basic understanding of end use (though you don't need to be an experienced sewist or quilter yourself), and to understand what buyers look for in prints and collections. Get to know the different manufacturers by visiting their websites. For a handy overview, look for the Fabric Manufacturer Guide on my blog, True Up (trueup.net/fabric-manufacturer-guide/).

Narrow your focus to companies that actually work with freelancers (a couple work exclusively with in-house designers). Evaluate their range of offerings. Do they have collections in a similar style to yours, or would yours stand out like a sore thumb? Do they seem to be targeting the type of person to whom your designs appeal? Are their collections put together in a standard way (with a focus print, secondary print, supporting prints), or are they more eclectic?

You don't necessarily need a fully developed portfolio of print-ready designs to start approaching quilting manufacturers. Some prefer to see just the seed of a collection, a few related designs or sketches. *They don't even have to be in repeat.* (These mock-ups, or *croquis* [page 71], enable artists to work out design ideas without getting too bogged down in the technicalities of repeats.) In fact, some manufacturers prefer that submissions *not* be in repeat, because it's easier to set them up themselves according to their mill's requirements. Others prefer layered vector art in repeat. Every company is a bit different, so contact the design director to ask about their submission guidelines.

Who you are can be as important as what you are designing; companies love it when you come with a built-in following. In general, if you're a fantastic artist with great ideas, and you're just what they were looking for to expand their catalog, they'll find a way to make it work no matter what your technical skill level is. That said, a well-thought-out presentation showing that you understand how prints and colorways work together, plus some mock-ups or actual projects using your digitally printed designs, will never hurt.

One final point of etiquette: Let companies know if you're submitting your designs to multiple places. Some companies meet on a fixed schedule to review submissions, but if they love your work, they want to know if they have to act quickly.

The trade show floor at the International Quilt Market, is held annually in Houston, Texas, each fall and in a different American city each spring.

What's in a Name? Naming Collections, Prints, and Colorways

Something as simple as the name of a print or colorway can make people take a second look and reconsider fabrics they would normally pass over. Some collections have made me turn up my nose at first, but after being hooked in by the names, I've learned about the idea behind the collection and have come to appreciate how the designer expressed that idea. Then I've turned around and bought the fabrics after all.

Names are hooks, so use them! Think of them as another design layer that helps tell the story behind the collection; express the idea; or pay tribute to a person, time, or event. In fact, sometimes a designer comes up with a name before the design itself, which is a great way of setting those self-imposed constraints we have discussed throughout this book.

OTHER LICENSING AVENUES

Many freelance textile designers license their work through agents. These agents range from the very narrowly specialized (prints for women's swimwear) to very broad (graphics and illustration for all kinds of markets). You might work on an assignment basis, or simply submit a portfolio of prints that are sold individually. Often, you have little or no control over the end product, and your contribution goes uncredited. But again, this varies depending on the situation. Still, if designing prints is the only part you care about, it's a great, and possibly lucrative, route to take. So how do you find an agent? Like sourcing converters, this is best done with old-school networking. Surtex, Printsource, and the Licensing Expo are three large trade shows devoted to art licensing. Plenty of information and advice for attending and exhibiting at these shows can be found online (see Resources, page 158).

Another option is to cut out the middleman and work directly with clients. It's like being a classic freelance graphic designer, only you happen to specialize in textile design. Of course, this route requires you to build a brand and to establish and maintain relationships with clients on your own (again, trade shows are your friends). But these direct relationships tend to lead to more collaboration and input regarding the final outcome of your work.

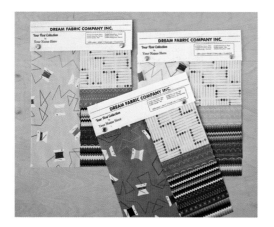

Fabric Design and the Big Picture

How big a role does fabric design play in your work or brand? What else helps pay the bills?

 I'm still in the beginning of my fabric design career, so it doesn't play a huge role at this point—it's just one of many things that I'm doing. I do think it's helping to build my brand, though. I also create surface designs that I sell and license to companies for other products besides fabric; I paint and illustrate and sell work on my online shop; I do some graphic design work (creating logos, custom patterns for websites, branding packages, etc.) for clients; and I sell my work in boutiques and shops around the country. —JESSICA LEVITT

 Designing fabric falls into my licensing income category, which is about 20–35 percent of my overall income to date. Other licensing income includes publishing (books, stationery) and quilts. Most of my income comes from quilts that we make in the studio. We've also just started printing and selling our own pattern line. —DENYSE SCHMIDT

With the release of my self-produced Monaco collection, fabric design and promotion has definitely been my main focus. When I'm not designing, I am packaging up orders or communicating with customers, figuring shipping rates, ordering supplies, developing advertising and PR, or working on projects and posting them on my blog. However, I have also done some work with stationery companies to use my prints on paper products, and I still fit in occasional freelance work when I can. —JENNIFER MOORE

 I also teach, and I write books and sewing patterns. But fabric design sets the stage for all of it. —BARI J. ACKERMAN

 Aside from designing fabric for Dotty Logic, I do private-label fabric design. It's great to collaborate with my clients and help them create their own one-of-a-kind fabric. I'm also a customer service and technical support representative for an electrical products manufacturer. Fabric design isn't a full-time job for me yet, and it may not be for many years—starting a new business takes a lot of time, energy, and brain cells! —JASONDA DESMOND

 Fabric design plays one of the largest roles in my creative life, but I love all aspects of surface design and I also love to paint. In addition to working with FreeSpirit, I work with other manufacturers to create scrapbooking products, stationery, rugs, and more. I also sell original paintings and prints of my work in my online shop. I look for every possible way to use my skills and creativity to bring in enough money to keep doing what I love. As far as paying the bills goes, one of the biggest earners for me has been placement of my paintings in corporate settings by fine-art consulting firms. —JENEAN MORRISON

 Fabric design is what I set out to do. Everything that comes after it is a happy accident. I have a pattern company, but again, it's really just a necessity to facilitate the fabric aspect of my business. I make the products to showcase the fabrics; when enough people asked for them, it just became silly to ignore that demand. —TULA PINK

 Fabric design is really the keynote of my brand. My sewing patterns are what initially started me in the industry, and the fabric was very close behind. These two pieces still remain the core of Amy Butler Design today and support each other beautifully. My fabric designs are the foundation for other aspects of my work, such as my bags, bedding, rugs, stationery, and wallpaper collections—so the initial art acts as a design hub for my entire brand. —AMY BUTLER

 Fabric designs are so important in my work. I'm picky about the fabrics I like, and my own designs are necessary in representing my brand, because surface pattern is my true passion. However, fabric design isn't my main source of income. I also sell my handmade toys and accessories online using the fabrics I love along with some of my own designs. And I submit a lot of my work to various greeting card and stationery companies. —ALICE BURROWS

 We each have other businesses that incorporate screen printing into objects ranging from children's clothing to housewares and accessories. Also, we both teach courses on design or fiber at local colleges.

—AROUNNA KHOUNNORAJ AND ROISIN FAGAN

Building Your Brand

To build your brand, you need to get your name "out there" and to present your designs and products in the most enticing, diverse ways possible.

Working the Room: Personal Brand Building

Many fabric designers come into the field by virtue of their fame in other arenas, such as Jay McCarroll (*Project Runway's* first-season winner), *Extreme Home Makeover* host Ty Pennington, and 70s icon Marie Osmond. Some designers enter the fabric world after building a name for themselves in other artistic areas, such as quilting, paper goods, fashion, interior design, or fine art. Unless you're one of these people, you have to build and promote your brand from the ground up.

Big-name fabric and textile designers have been around since William Morris in the late 1800s, but Amy Butler really launched the modern era of celebrity designers. Her fabrics and patterns were a breath of fresh air at the turn of the twenty-first century and filled a design void for a new generation of sewers. Today, nearly every new designer follows her business model. She regularly produces beautiful fabric collections, sewing patterns, books, finished textile products, wallpaper, stationery, and more. Most importantly, she's a wonderful, warm, engaging person for whom giving back to her community is a top priority.

Simply having your name out there and letting people get to know you is half the battle. *You*—not your professionally designed logo or line of products—are the brand. You're not forming relationships with people just so they'll buy your fabrics. Fabric is not a hugely lucrative business for most designers, but connecting with so many friendly, inspiring people more than makes up for it. Simply putting your smiling face out there in the community makes people sit up and take notice when your name is attached to something. When people know you or are acquainted with an aspect of your life, they begin to see your products on a deeper level, more personally. Your designs are an extension of you, your personality, your identity, your story.

Fortunately, the Internet makes it a cinch to tell your story. It's unusual these days for a designer *not* to have a website or blog, or to be active on the latest social networking site. In fact, several new rising stars in the fabric design world first built a following through their blogs. So if you don't already have a blog, *get one now*. Write about your inspiration, your creative process, your daily triumphs and tribulations. It can be personal or you can keep it strictly professional.

Conventional wisdom on building blog readership used to be to comment frequently on the blogs of bigger fish and to cold-email to suggest link exchanges. Now, so many microcommunities are on the web that it's much easier to find your niche and grow organically—to be "famous for 15 minutes," as the modern twist on Andy Warhol's quote goes. The new way is to chat on Twitter; lead or participate in swaps, sew-alongs, and competitions; trade advice on forums; and share interesting links. And, of course, to have a blog that people love to read. Your online life should be its own reward, not the means to an end.

There's still no substitute for meeting people in person. Join (or start!) local quilt guilds and craft groups. Teach your skills to others. Attend trade shows. In the retail fabric market, the biggest trade show is the International Quilt Market, which the company Quilts Inc. holds in Houston, Texas, each fall and in a different American city each spring. To obtain admission as a prospective designer, contact Quilts Inc. for specific requirements.

Marketing: Beyond Yardage

Avenues to successful marketing of your fabric designs include additional products, stellar presentation through samples and great photography, and creating a buzz with publicity.

SAMPLES

Aside from personal brand building, the best way to increase interest in and sales of your fabric is to *show people how to use it*. How many times have you shrugged your shoulders upon seeing a certain fabric on the bolt or in a 2″ swatch on the Internet, only to be totally smitten by it upon seeing it in a quilt or garment?

Showing sample products that incorporate your fabric is a must. Many designers and manufacturers routinely offer free patterns for these items. If you can't design or sew or don't have friends or family to pitch in to help, consider outsourcing. Many quilt and sewing pattern designers out there look for ways to promote their brand. Cast your net for people who sew for hire.

Another option is to fake it with a technique called photo draping. Image editing programs have tools that allow you to overlay a digital fabric swatch onto an existing image (say, of a model in a dress, or of a nicely styled couch with pillows), then warp and add perspective so that the textiles in the original photo look like they're made of the fabric.

PATTERNS AND PRODUCTS

Many fabric designers, especially in the quilting world, also produce sewing or quilt patterns. This provides another income stream, and the fabric and patterns help sell one another.

But not everyone sews. Offering products for sale that are made with your fabrics, even if they're simple—such as tote bags or pillows—opens up your market to more potential customers.

Patterns from various designers

Again, if you can't take on the production yourself, consider outsourcing. A great source of information on manufacturing is the book *The Entrepreneur's Guide to Sewn Product Manufacturing,* by Kathleen Fasanella, and her website, fashion-incubator.com (see Resources, page 158). Remember, though, that some buyers will use your fabrics to sell their own goods. Some designers think that this dilutes their brand; others embrace it as a brand expander. If you prefer having total control over how your fabrics are presented to the world, then don't sell your fabrics at all but focus on sewn products.

THE ART OF PHOTOGRAPHING FABRIC

Another must is beautiful product photography. Digital single-lens reflex (DSLR) cameras are very affordable these days and allow you to change lenses for different types of shots. You can create a "studio" for low-light situations with white paper or fabric backdrops and a few lights. Close-up (macro) shots of your fabric show potential customers its weave and texture even if they can't touch it. If you're selling via the Internet or by mail, it's vital to provide a good representation of the print's colors and scale. The standard for representing a print's scale is a shot or scan with a ruler or coin, but I find sewn product shots or images of stacked bolts or rolls far more helpful. Why not include them all in your promotional materials?

The more views, the better. If you don't know much about photography, read up on the subject, take a class, or scour the Internet for instruction.

If you follow the personal brand-building advice in this section, you may be lucky to find that "viral marketing" sends you as much (or more!) business than you can handle. But more often than not, it's beneficial to promote yourself and your products the old-fashioned way, through press releases or press kits. Submit your biographical information, and information about your company and your latest fabrics, to magazines, newspapers, blogs, podcasts, and even design-oriented cable TV stations. Follow each media outlet's submission guidelines. Include swatches and copies of any free or paid sewing patterns. Then, make it easy for interested outlets to cover you. Create a "press center" on your website with a variety of beautiful, print-resolution photos that editors can download and use in their publications.

Going Pro: Should You Go to School?

I am occasionally asked whether it's necessary to have a degree in textile design to design fabric prints. The answer is a resounding no: In fact, I wrote this book so that anyone can learn the basics. That said, I would strongly encourage anyone to enroll in a textile design program. You will be mentored at every stage by instructors who have extensive experience in the industry, you'll be surrounded by inspiration, and you'll have access to resources and archives that the rest of us only dream of. You'll gain in-depth technical knowledge of the printing process and hone your point of view as an artist. (For a list of prestigious textile design programs, see Resources, page 158.)

Keep in mind that fabric printing is only a subset of the textile industry. A degree program will also expose you to many other areas. It's difficult to learn about subjects such as woven textile design and textile engineering outside of universities.

Career Paths

Professional textile designers may work for a retail fabric company or, more likely, for a company that produces specific types of apparel or home décor products. Many work on a freelance basis for several companies. Day-to-day work might involve designing unique patterns or setting up repeats for or coloring others' designs. Some designers work directly with mills on quality assurance, even visiting mills in person to oversee production. Work may focus on the surface pattern or may also include design, styling, or marketing of the finished goods. Because so much of production—including a good portion of design jobs—has moved overseas, the current landscape is highly competitive. As in any field, however, talent rises to the top, especially if it is paired with strong technical knowledge.

Meet the Roundtable Designers

Photo by Bari J. Ackerman

Bari J. Ackerman started her Bari J. brand of handbags and accessories in 2004 and turned the focus to fabric and sewing pattern design five years later after the debut of her first fabric collection for Windham Fabrics. She currently designs fabric for Lecien and is also the author of the book *Inspired to Sew* by Bari J.

barijonline.com

Photo by Andrew Bencsko III

Michelle Engel Bencsko worked for more than a decade as a design director in the apparel industry before launching her freelance career as a fabric designer. In 2009, along with partner Gina Pantastico, she launched Cloud9 Fabrics, a company producing colorful, modern organic print collections for the quilting and crafts market.

cloud9fabrics.com

Photo by Stacey Hedman

Melissa Averinos designs wild, funky, graphic collections for Andover Fabrics. She is also an author (*Small Stash Sewing: 24 Projects Using Designer Fat Quarters*), painter, and owner of the shop Yummy Goods in Cape Cod, Massachusetts.

www.yummygoods.com

Photo by Alice Burrows

Alice Burrows creates handmade toys from 1960s–70s vintage fabric and from her own fabrics inspired by that era, which she prints digitally. She lives on the South Devon coast in the U.K.

aliceapple.co.uk

Photo by David Bedell

Mo Bedell is a freelance graphic and apparel designer. Her fabric collections for Blue Hill Fabrics are pretty and feminine with a modern edge.

limegardenias.blogspot.com

Photo by David Butler

Amy Butler ushered in a new era of contemporary fabric design when she released her first collections in the first few years of the twenty-first century. She is known for blending a wide variety of influences to create lush, beautiful, and distinctive designs. She is also a prolific designer of sewing patterns and author of several sewing and lifestyle books. In addition, she licenses designs for textiles, accessories, and stationery, and even launched a line of yarn and knitting patterns with Rowan in 2010.

amybutlerdesign.com

Photo by Jasonda Desmond

Jasonda Desmond is an illustrator and freelance textile designer who founded her organic fabric and home accessories brand, Dotty Logic, in 2010. She prints her fresh, modern graphic collections digitally and offers them for sale through Etsy.

jasonda.com

Photo by Heidi Kenney

Heidi Kenney is a Pennsylvania-based artist and crafter-at-large best known for her whimsical plush toys. She has brought her characters to fabric through digital printing; she's also the author of *Every Day's a Holiday: Year-Round Crafting With Kids*.

mypapercrane.com

Photo by Natalie Grummer

Josephine Kimberling is a licensing artist who has worked extensively in the fashion and stationery industries. Her keen eye for fashion and color is evident in her several fabric collections for Robert Kaufman Fabrics.

josephinekimberling.com

Photo by Jessica Levitt

Jessica Levitt has designed several lines of fabric for Windham Fabrics. You can see her latest projects and catch up on her life at her blog.

juicy-bits.typepad.com

Photo by Heather Moore

Heather Moore is a textile designer from South Africa. Under her brand, Skinny LaMinx, she creates textiles, ceramics, and fabrics for the home, often based on her Scandinavian-modern-inspired papercut designs. She also designs organic quilting-weight collections for Cloud9 Fabrics.

skinnylaminx.com

Photo by David Miguelucci

Jennifer Moore founded her company, Monaluna, in 2005. She has designed collections for Robert Kaufman Fabrics and Birch Fabrics. She also self-produces organic cotton fabrics under the Monaluna name. Simple dots, juvenile novelties, and sophisticated florals let her fresh, retro-modern design voice shines through.

monaluna.com

Photo by Joel T. Rose

Jenean Morrison is a surface designer and painter from Memphis, Tennessee. She has licensed her work for stationery, rugs, and kitchenware, and she designs fabric collections for FreeSpirit Fabrics. She is known for her complex, layered, graphic, yet bohemian, style.

jeneanmorrison.net

Photo by Tula Pink

Tula Pink's fabrics are famous for causing viewers to do double takes. Her fabric collections for Moda and FreeSpirit Fabrics are each lush, colorful, alternate universes unto their own, filled with fantastic creatures and hidden pictures.

tulapink.com

Photo by John Booth

Photo by Roisin Fagan

Repeat Studio is a collaboration between Canadians Arounna Khounnoraj and Roisin Fagan. Their hand-screen-printed fabrics feature sparse, beautiful motifs. Fagan is a textile designer and teacher who also owns the textile studio Bespoke Uprising. Khournnoraj, along with her husband, John Booth, runs a multidisciplinary studio and brick-and-mortar shop called Bookhou, located in Toronto.

repeatstudio.com

Photo by Lane duPont

Denyse Schmidt is a quilter known for blending the traditional and modern, resulting in quilts that are offbeat yet sparse and sophisticated. She is also an author (*Denyse Schmidt Quilts: 30 Colorful Quilt and Patchwork Projects*), teacher, and quilt pattern designer. Her vintage-inspired fabric collections are produced by FreeSpirit Fabrics.

dsquilts.com

Photo by Ryan Swift

Jessica Swift is a surface pattern designer, artist, and designer. In addition to licensing work to clients, she also offers prints, cards, and more through her own online shop. Her modern, fashion-forward fabric collections are produced by Red Rooster Fabrics.

jessicaswift.com

Photo provided by designer

Photo provided by designer

Umbrella Prints is a hand-screen-printed fabric design label founded by Australians Amy Prior and Carly Schwerdt. They produce a mix of graphic and organic hand-drawn prints in a fresh, compelling palette. The two also run Nest Studio, a shop/studio that offers art classes for children.

umbrellaprints.com.au

Resources

Further Reading

Adobe Illustrator CS5 Classroom in a Book
and **Adobe Photoshop CS5 Classroom in a Book**
by Adobe Creative Team (Adobe Press, 2010)

Adobe Photoshop for Textile Design
(for Adobe Photoshop CS5)
by Frederick L. Chipkin (self-published, 2010)

> A great source for learning how to work with
> scanned color artwork (for example, paintings or
> vintage textiles). The author also has books on tex-
> tile design in Photoshop Elements and GIMP.

All About Silk: A Fabric Dictionary & Swatchbook
All About Cotton: A Fabric Dictionary & Swatchbook
All About Wool: A Fabric Dictionary & Swatchbook
by Julie Parker's Fabric Reference Series (Rain City
Publishing; 1991, 1993, 1996 respectively)

Art Cloth: A Guide to Surface Design for Fabric
by Jane Dunnewold (Interweave Press, 2010)

> The bible for printing with dyes and for many
> other free-form surface design techniques.

**Bend the Rules with Fabric: Fun Sewing Projects with
Stencils, Stamps, Dye, Photo Transfers, Silk Screening,
and More** by Amy Karol (Potter Craft, 2009)

**Color: A Course in Mastering the Art of Mixing
Colors** by Betty Edwards (Tarcher, 2004)

Confessions of a First Timer by Khristian A. Howell
(self-published ebook, 2010)

> All about exhibiting at Surtex, one of the premier
> trade shows for licensing surface pattern designs.
> (khristianahowell.com/shop/ebooks/confessions)

Dating Fabrics: A Color Guide 1800–1960 by Eileen
Jahnke Trestain (American Quilter's Society, 1998)

Dating Fabrics 2: A Color Guide 1950–2000
by Eileen Jahnke Trestain (American
Quilter's Society, 2005)

Digital Textile Design by Melanie Bowles and
Ceri Isaac (Laurence King Publishers, 2009)

**The Entrepreneur's Guide to Sewn Product
Manufacturing** by Kathleen Fasanella
(Apparel Technical Services, 1998)

**From Fiber to Fabric: The Essential Guide to
Quiltmaking Textiles** by Harriet Hargrave
(C&T Publishing, 1997; available as ebook or
Print on Demand only)

**Pattern Design and Beyond: An Insider's Guide to
Creating and Managing Your Own Surface Design
Career** by Claudia Brown and Jessie Whipple Vickery
of Pattern People (self-published ebook, 2011)

> A great source for learning about licensing,
> designed for agents and print studios.
> (patternpeople.com/ebook)

Principles of Pattern Design by Richard M.
Proctor (Dover Publications, 1990)

**Surface Pattern Design: A Handbook of How
to Create Decorative and Repeat Patterns for
Designers and Students** by V. Ann Waterman
(Hastings House Publishers, 1984)

**Textile Designs: Two Hundred Years of European
and American Patterns Organized by Motif,
Style, Color, Layout, and Period** by Susan Meller
and Joost Elffers (Harry N. Abrams, 2002)

Twentieth-Century Pattern Design by Lesley
Jackson (Princeton Architectural Press, 2007)

Supplies

Dharma Trading Company

dharmatrading.com

Textile printing and dyeing supply superstore; has the web's largest selection of PFD fabrics.

Dick Blick

dickblick.com

Art supply superstore; has a wide selection of block-printing supplies.

G&S Dye

gsdye.com

Toronto-based textile design supply house—they know their stuff when it comes to textile printing.

Jacquard Silk Connection

silkconnection.com

PFD fabrics

McClain's Printmaking Supplies

imcclains.com

Printmaking supply specialty store

Pocono Mt. Screen Supply

poconoscreen.com

Screen-printing supplies. The most affordable place I've found for custom-sized screens (up to 60″ × 60″).

Ryonet

ryonet.com

Screen-printing supplies and tons of how-to videos

Screen Printing Superstore

screenprintingsupplies.com

Full selection of supplies; will mix inks according to your chosen Pantone color.

Thai Silks

thaisilks.com

PFD silks and blank clothing and accessories

Victory Factory

victoryfactory.com

Screen-printing supplies, including water-based textile inks

Software

Adobe Photoshop and Illustrator

adobe.com

Artlandia SymmetryWorks and SymmetryShop

(plugins for Adobe Photoshop and Illustrator)
artlandia.com

Fabric Studio

thefabstudio.com

Fashion Toolbox

fashiontoolbox.com

GIMP (the GNU Image Manipulation Program)
gimp.org

Inkscape

inkscape.org

Digital Textile Print Bureaus

Fabric on Demand

fabricondemand.com

Various cottons, linen blends, and synthetics, like spandex

First2Print

first2print.com

Higher-end digital textile printing bureau. It offers acid, reactive, and disperse dyes on dozens of fabrics.

Karma Kraft

karmakraft.com

One of the few affordably priced printers that uses reactive dyes, which are more wash-fast than pigment inks.

S. C. Fabric Printing

scfabricprinting.com

Pigment and reactive dye printing starting at $25/yard

Spoonflower

spoonflower.com

First and largest affordably priced digital textile printing service. Offers ever-widening variety of base cloths, as well as weekly contests and a thriving marketplace in which you can sell your fabrics.

Stoff'n

stoffn.de

Based in Germany, this service ships throughout Europe. (German-language based)

Stoff-Schmie.de

stoff-schmie.de

Based in Germany and ships throughout Europe, prints with reactive dyes. (German-language based)

Trade Shows

International Quilt Festival (Quilts, Inc.)
quilts.com

Licensing International Expo
licensingexpo.com

Printsource New York
printsourcenewyork.com

Surtex
surtex.com

Undergraduate Textile Design Degree Programs

California School of Professional Fabric Design (Berkeley, CA)
fabricschool.com

Fashion Institute of Design & Merchandising
(four campuses in California)
fidm.edu/majors/textile-design

Fashion Institute of Technology
(New York, NY)
fitnyc.edu

North Carolina State University
(Raleigh, NC)
www.tx.ncsu.edu

Philadelphia University
philau.edu/designandmedia; click
Design Programs > Textile Design

Rhode Island School of Design
(Providence, RI)
risd.edu

Savannah College of Art & Design
(Savannah, GA, and other campuses)
scad.edu

Websites

Art Licensing Blog
artlicensingblog.com

How to break into and survive the art licensing world, written by Tara Reed.

Color Theory
worqx.com/color/index.htm

An accessible overview of color theory.

GigPosters
gigposters.com

A screen-printing community site, focused on rock posters and T-shirts; forum has screen-printing information.

Pantone
pantone.com

Not only the place to purchase Pantone products, but to join their community of designers for technical support and inspiration.

Surface Design Association
surfacedesign.org

Toronto Fashion Incubator
fashionincubator.com

A treasure trove of information for those seeking to get into sewn product manufacturing.

True Up's Fabric Printing Forum
trueup.net/forum

A companion forum/community to this book. Ask questions, share tips and inspiration, and connect with other talented designers.

Wet Canvas
wetcanvas.com

A huge artists' forum with thriving printmaking and fiber arts communities.

About the Author

Photo by Jennifer Ramos

Kim Kight has been obsessed with fabric, and especially fabric print design, since receiving a sewing machine as a gift from her mother-in-law in 2000. She established the blog True Up in 2008 to share that obsession with the world. Along the way, she taught herself fabric design, and now teaches classes on the subject in Austin, Texas, where she lives with her husband and two sons.